A Financial Planning Model for
Private Colleges: A Research Report

A Financial Planning Model

For Private Colleges

A Research Report

William J. Arthur

University Press of Virginia

Charlottesville

STUDIES IN BUSINESS ADMINISTRATION
The publication of this study has been assisted by the
Tayloe Murphy Institute and the Graduate School of
Business Administration of the University of Virginia.

THE UNIVERSITY PRESS OF VIRGINIA

First published 1973

ISBN: 0-8139-0409-9
Library of Congress Catalog Card Number: 72-92879
Printed in the United States of America

Contents

Foreword

MOST nonprofit educational institutions have two primary objectives—an educational objective and a financial objective. The latter may be as simple as to break even or to remain solvent, or it may be stated as a complex financial position that the institution wishes to achieve, or maintain, in order to support its projected future activities. The educational and financial objectives do not generally lead in the same direction, at least not in the short run. Improving educational programs is expensive, and reduction of expenditures tends to threaten educational quality. The university's administrators continually have to balance financial capacity and educational desires to achieve an optimum result.

Because they are educational institutions, their educational objectives quite naturally tend to attract the greatest attention. The quality of an institution is measured in terms of its educational achievements, not in terms of financial success. In fact, the recent deficits at prestigious universities are described more as noble sacrifices to a higher cause than as evidence of some kind of unsatisfactory performance. To end the year with a surplus these days is a bit shameful, not a matter for public crowing, and certainly not for the ears of those loyal alumni whose continued support is urgently needed.

For a good many years, and for most institutions, the financial objective has played a secondary role in determining plans and actions. For some it simply defined the pool of funds, hoped to become a bit larger each year, from which the academicians could draw to support educational activities. For these institutions, as Howard Bowen has said, "the basic principle of college finance is very simple. Institutions raise as much money as they can get and spend it all."[1]

In recent years the picture has changed for many institutions. The pool of funds has slowed its rate of increase, or has even begun a decline. Costs, on the other hand, have kept on rising for what seem

[1] Howard R. Bowen, "Financial Needs of the Campus," in Academy of Political Science, *The Corporation and the Campus: Corporate Support of Higher Education in the 1970's* (New York, 1970) , p. 81.

to be legitimate and irreversible reasons. The 1970 Carnegie Commission on Higher Education study estimated that 61 percent of all institutions of higher education, with 78 percent of the total enrollment, were either in financial difficulty or headed for financial trouble. For private institutions the picture was even worse, for the estimates showed 72 percent of the institutions with 88 percent of the enrollment in these two categories. Thirty percent of the private institutions with 47 percent of the enrollment were estimated to be already in financial difficulty. Earl Cheit defined these conditions as "a new depression in higher education."[2]

For the first time many educational institutions are being forced to cut, usually just services, but occasionally whole programs. Unpleasant trade-offs are required of university administrators, in which both financial and educational implications must be weighed. Whereas some years ago planning errors could fairly easily be absorbed in an institution's growth, this luxury no longer exists. Planning must be more precise, in both the educational and financial areas.

New tools are needed to meet these increased requirements for financial and educational planning. These should be planning tools, not more hand-wringing ways to explain how an institution got into financial difficulty. In short, we do not need another look to the rear, but instead a clearer vision ahead.

Mr. Arthur's study is aimed at such a forward look. He accepted the financial pinch as given, and spent his research effort devising an approach to handle it.

What he presents is an analytical approach to the long-range planning function. He describes a systematic way of pulling together the diverse elements of an educational institution so that planning can be effective. Then he suggests a way of defining and organizing the relevant planning data so that top administrators can exert knowledgeable control over their institution's destiny.

As he notes in the latter part of the book, his approach is less useful in large universities, especially those that are decentralized in their administration or have large nontuition income. This is true partly because Mr. Arthur's approach focuses on tuition income and partly because such complex institutions present enormous difficulties for any planning process. There are, nevertheless, a large number of colleges and universities for which his suggested framework would appear to be a potentially useful planning tool.

[2] Earl F. Cheit, *The New Depression in Higher Education: A Study of Financial Conditions at 41 Colleges and Universities* (New York: McGraw Hill, 1971).

In his research Mr. Arthur did not stop at merely devising what ought to be a helpful approach to planning. He went on first to evaluate its feasibility at several test schools and then actually to put it in use at one of the colleges he had studied. The test showed that once the approach was understood and the data were at hand, steps that represented considerable accomplishments in themselves, college administrators could use his analytical approach to gain important insights into the implications of their planning options.

Such a planning framework is not in itself a solution to the financial problems of higher education. The solution will come only through actions that either increase revenue or reduce expenses. However, Mr. Arthur's proposals facilitate the kind of clear articulation of intentions and costs that will enable administrators to see their way to making the best possible decisions under difficult circumstances.

William Rotch

Charlottesville, Virginia
June 1972

Preface

SINCE World War II higher education in the United States has attracted students in vastly larger numbers than ever before anywhere in the world. As a people, we have realized the virtue of an educated citizenry, and as we often do, we have overindulged. In recent years our excesses have brought about a sobering appraisal of the financial consequences. We now hear people question whether we can afford the massive system of higher education we have developed. From the opposite point of view, others argue that we cannot afford *not* to educate our people, and they echo Jefferson's thought that we cannot be both ignorant and free.

Without entering into the debate over the need for education, and accepting the present expensiveness of highr education, many people, including the writer, have concerned themselves with the question of how best to cope with the massive financial commitment we have made and are making to higher education. Several basic themes move through conversations on the financial woes of colleges and universities: the basic function of education is a concept that is difficult to measure; it is difficult to retreat after commitments are made to educational programs; an early warning system might be helpful in controlling expenditures; perhaps some of the experience of industry could be useful in administering higher education; and finally, we need a system.

It is natural that someone who has spent time in both worlds— industry and higher education—would become curious about the validity of these themes. I proposed to a number of funding agencies that a study be made and that a financial planning model be developed that drew on the industry experience without infringing upon the historic academic integrity of teachers and institutions. The study was further encouraged by the dean and the faculty of the University of Virginia Graduate School of Business Administration by allowing it to meet my disseratation requirements.

This research was accomplished under the direction of Professor William Rotch at the Graduate School of Business Administration, University of Virginia. His patient criticism and suggestions have been invaluable in focusing my thoughts and in the presentation of the research findings. In addition, other members of the Graduate Business School faculty were helpful to this work. Dean Charles C. Abbott had many helpful comments to make at the proposal defense and as the research progressed. Also, Professor Almond R. Coleman, Professor Lee R. Johnston, Professor Frederick S. Morton, and Professor John L. Colley, Jr., offered numerous suggestions that helped to break loose particularly knotty problems during the study.

The original research for this book was conducted under a research grant from U.S. Office of Education, Grant no. OEG–3–9–080063–0001.

W. J. A.

Jacksonville, Florida
June 1972

A Financial Planning Model for
Private Colleges: A Research Report

CHAPTER I

Statement of the Problem

M UCH attention has been given recently to the many problems facing administrators in higher education. One of the most significant issues, and the one dealt with here, concerns the most effective methods of utilizing the financial resources of private schools. During a period in which the need for more and more educational opportunities has become evident, we have had strong inflationary trends in college and university operating costs along with increasing difficulty in raising the income flow. New sources of income have been hard to identify. All these pressures have forced administrators to make hard decisions concerning the feasibility of new academic programs. In a frequently hostile environment college presidents, vice-presidents, and deans have had to balance anticipated income against costs that were committed considerably in advance of the receipt of income. The specific objective of this study is to provide a systematic approach to guide administrators in the trade-off process of arriving at the institution's package of academic programs.

Consultants, educational researchers, and middle-level administrators have made many attempts to resolve the dilemma, to provide a model for confronting academic needs with financial feasibility. There is still a need, however, for a systematic approach to assessing feasibility and for a simple measurement of the institution's ability to support an agreed-upon package of programs.

Many techniques have been suggested to guide administrators as they attempt to lead their institutions to think about the future, and these include a variety of planning models, some of which have been adapted to computer application. For instance, one such model compares the institution to a composite or "average" school in its category. The comparison is based on a vast array of statistical characteristics, with an apparent tendency to have all the factors analyzed by the model approach some norm.

Before these models are used, administrators should ask who decided on the norms and whether all schools should aspire toward the same characteristics. Private schools already tend to mimic the offerings of state-supported institutions too much, and small schools are trying too hard to compete with big universities and "be all things to all people." The comparative model and others examined contribute to the tendency to justify whatever is done rather than to provide avenues for restricting programs or for identifying the financial means of pursuing innovation in programs. Most damaging, however, is the tendency of top administrators to supplant their judgment with mechanical processes of computers or "middle-level" planners.

Perhaps the telling indictment of recent models is that their output is usually a massive computer print-out or a voluminous narrative that takes more time to study than most top administrators can spare. Also, the data provided are frequently of more interest to middle-level administrators such as admissions directors, registrars, business officers, and perhaps deans of schools within a multiunit institution. The top administrators—the president, the vice-presidents, the chancellors, or whatever the title may be—are still left to determine what all the statistics mean to the total institutional program with no means of evaluation except their own subjective attitudes.

What they need is a relatively simple measurement that can tell them whether financial resources will support the myriad of plans offered from lower levels. The model presented here is intended to do this. First there is a verbal model which outlines a framework for institutional planning, then a quantitative model which relates the plans to financial constraints, and finally a mathematical measurement which top administrators can use to evaluate the plans. The model draws from emerging concepts of business strategy formulation as well as from program planning–budgeting techniques developed in the federal government, particularly in the Department of Defense.

The need for long-range planning is not questioned; indeed, it is critical to higher education. This need stems first from the high proportion of costs that result from long-term commitments. For instance, faculty salaries can represent a substantial commitment for many years into the future because of current interpretations of academic tenure. Unlike industry, curtailment of an activity in an educational institution does not mean the termination of the employment of people associated with that activity. College administrators usually cannot even evaluate all units of their academic organization until a crisis situation is at hand, although the business manager is able to evaluate units on a systematic basis. In addition, there are many expenses incurred in support of the faculty that tend not to vary with the level of either student enrollment or other income sources. These committed costs cannot be controlled by annual budgets but must be planned before they are incurred.

Because of particular limitations on financial resources, long-range planning is vital for private colleges so that new programs can be seen in the context of financial constraints. Both state-supported and private institutions receive tuition income, gifts, grants, and endowment income. But private colleges at this date seldom have direct access to state revenues. The proportion of rapidly rising expenditures not supported by nontuition income in private colleges must be paid by student charges. This situation indicates that private colleges must have better information in advance to plan financial commitments if they are to survive the challenge of state-supported education.

As part of the long-range planning process, a quantitative measurement is needed to evaluate financial performance. This should not be construed as a need for a measurement of educational objectives, but colleges and universities do have financial objectives apart from the academic purposes.[1] It is in the evaluation of these financial objectives that the lack of a quantitative measurement is crucial. When all the diverse plans have been accumulated, top administrators still have to consider whether the institution has the financial means in the long run to support the whole package. There is no existing single measure of financial feasibility that can be used to plan or control operating and capital expenditures. This situation contrasts with that in industry, where numerous quantitative measures are in use. For colleges and universities, however, there are no production standards, no "percent of market" goals, no current ratios or receivable and inventory-turnover ratios, and most importantly, no rate of return on investment.

Interestingly enough, in recent years, managers as well as writers in business have come to recognize that the return-on-investment (ROI) goal is not always the most appropriate means of evaluating performance even in their world. For instance, the profit motive for a research and development function is often too remote to stimulate the scientists and engineers; a stenographic pool in a major corporation is little concerned about ROI; and many capital expenditures, such as air conditioning for the plant and office, do not have the direct purpose of providing an ROI.

As a result, the concept of "management by objective" has de-

[1] Faculty or course evaluations are not the subject of this research report; yet one cannot observe the plight of higher education without feeling that some form of evaluation by administrators in good faith would improve the organizational relationships that have been strained in recent years.

veloped, and certain techniques have emerged that can be of value to administrators in higher education. These techniques involve determining manageable segments of the institutional mission; segments that can be analyzed more objectively than the broad statement of the total mission.

C. E. Graese, partner in Peat, Marwick, Mitchell and Company, has described existing administrative practices in higher education: "Educational institutions must continue to be classed among the more backward of organizations insofar as administrative procedures are concerned. Tradition has tended to rule. Vast quantities of new monies are being invested in educational plant, equipment, and techniques, but on the basis of academic programs and approaches already obsolete."[2] His company is one of a number of organizations that have devised heuristic or computerized mathematical models to assist higher education.

A number of foundations, including the Danforth and the Ford foundations, have expressed much dissatisfaction with the financial management techniques used by private colleges today.[3] Many writers also have pointed out the need for planning and for long-range views of the financial structure of colleges and universities, but few have presented effective methods by which colleges might use long-range planning measures to evaluate the long-range financial implications of specific proposals for new programs and projects. A method will be proposed here for spanning this gap in the practices of private colleges and universities.

The Research Methodology

A word should be said about the research scope and techniques used to develop the proposed model. The original research was directed toward two interrelated purposes:

1. To examine the system by which private colleges and universities manage their long-range expenditures and to compare this system with the process of managing capital expenditures in industry, and,

2. To develop a methodology, including a quantitative measurement, to evaluate the financial ability of private institutions to accomplish their objectives. It was envisioned that this quanti-

[2] Graese, "University Management—A Total Review," *Management Controls* (house organ of Peat, Marwick, Mitchell & Company), April 1968, pp. 75–76.

[3] *Chronicle of Higher Education*, II, no. 12 (Feb. 26, 1968), article quoting McGeorge Bundy, president of the Ford Foundation.

tative measure would facilitate a computerized model that would allow top administrators to answer the "what if" questions that come to the front in long-range planning.

Although this report does not make direct conclusions concerning the first purpose, the comparison with industry methods permeates the entire discussion. Further, the organizational analysis leading to the presentation of the model is focused by an extensive comparison with business organizational concepts.

Profitability is a motivating objective in industry and the rates of ROI measure the degree to which segments of the business, as well as the entire business, are accomplishing the objectives. The methodology referred to in the second purpose is also intended to measure the ability of the colleges and universities to accomplish their objectives, but these objectives are related to liquidity and ultimately to solvency rather than profitability, for profitability is a meaningless factor for educational institutions.

The methodology proposed in this study is in the form of a three-stage model: (1) the identification of institutional strategies, (2) the classification of operating and capital expenditures by strategies, and (3) a quantitative measure of the financial ability of the institution to accomplish the strategies. The model is to be used to evaluate future plans before financial commitments are made to new programs or projects; it is not intended to be a means of evaluating past performance of the institution or any part thereof.

The first step in developing the methodology was to identify concrete statements of objectives less abstract than the usual statements of broad mission. The schools at which the research was conducted had objectives identified in varying degrees of specificity, but none had made them explicit to the campus community. There were no realistic objectives in terms of the utilization of available resources or the environmental constraints on private higher education. Therefore, as a starting point, it was necessary to devise a framework that would help break up the broad missions into identifiable components that could be measured in terms of financial feasibility.

The long-range expenditure commitments in higher education include more than capital expenditures for buildings, equipment, and fixtures. Certain expenses normally referred to in industry as operating expenses are long-term commitments in higher education. For this reason any proposed measurement had to apply to expenditures of both types—capital expenditures and operating expenditures.

The proposed methodology is expected to be useful to top administrators in evaluating the financial feasibility of allocations of future resources and in testing the feasibility of such strategies before commitments are made. Once the broad strategic plans have been developed at the policy-making level, they can then be given to the "middle management" group to fill in the details of operating, capital, and cash budgets. This latter phase is usually the object of most of the models being publicized today, such as the Resource Requirement Prediction Model developed by the National Center for Higher Education Management Systems at WICHE.

The research was conducted in the following sequence:

1. The policies and procedures for financial administration at Brunther College[4] were examined through interviews with the administrators and through analysis of financial records and reports.
2. The three-stage financial planning model was devised and applied to Brunther College. Inputs for the model were determined from the records and source documents at the college.
3. The policies and procedures for financial administration at three test schools were determined and compared with the Brunther findings.
4. The systems in the three schools were compared with the industry practices for managing capital expenditures, determined from a survey of the business finance literature.
5. The availability of the data for the three-stage model was determined at the test schools.
6. A test of the usefulness was made at Brunther College by holding a meeting of top administrators where the model was discussed and used to demonstrate its application to long-range decision-making.
7. As a result of the test at Brunther and the tests for availability of inputs at the three test schools, one further research step was taken at a large private university. The previous work indicated a need to determine the effects on the model of larger size and organizational complexity, and both were studied at the major university.

In summary, the research was conducted by first developing the model at Brunther College and then testing the results at four other institutions. These were selected to represent a spectrum of characteristics such as total size, endowment size, age, organization, growth trends, geography, major source of income, church or other affiliation, institutional objectives, and administrative competence and

---

[4] The names of the institutions participating in this study have been disguised to avoid singling any one of them out as an example of either good or bad administrative practices.

attitude. The purpose was not to determine the effect of any one of these characteristics on the three-stage model but only to assure that the model had more general application than to Brunther College alone.

The research design seemed to call for the answer to a number of questions about each of the two purposes of the study. These questions are:

I. For comparison of the management processes
 A. At Brunther College
 1. What are the financial objectives of the college?
 2. Who in the college organization has responsibility for
 a. Initiating new ideas for programs and projects
 b. Evaluating expenditure requests
 c. Approving expenditure requests
 d. Implementing the programs or projects requested
 3. What policies and procedures are in use at the college to carry out the steps in administering long-range financial commitments?
 4. Identify and define the characteristics of Brunther College as to size, age, growth trends, endowment size, amount of nontuition income, organization, church or other affiliation, institutional objectives, and administrative competence and attitude
 B. At other private colleges and universities
 1. Identify and define the same characteristics listed above
 2. How do the financial objectives, policies, and procedures compare to those at Brunther College?
 3. How do the organizational structures compare to that at Brunther College?
 C. General
 1. What are the similarities between the system in the five participating institutions for administering long-term financial commitments and the process in industry for managing capital expenditures?
 2. Is the industry process applicable, in whole or in part, to the needs of higher education as evidenced by the five schools?
II. For development of the three-stage model
 A. At Brunther College
 1. Is there an existing analytical technique used at the college to evaluate long-range financial commitments? If so, what is it and how is it used?
 2. Is the proposed model applicable to Brunther College's

need for financial planning information and can it be a
useful guide to top administrators in long-range planning?

B. At other colleges and universities

   1. Is there an existing analytical technique in use at the
four test schools to evaluate long-range financial commitments? If so, what is it and how is it used?

   2. Are the inputs necessary for the three-stage model available in the proper form at other schools?

     a. Are the administrators able to identify strategies?

     b. Are the necessary financial data in the proper form?

     c. Do the schools have the staff competence and organi-
zational structure necessary to implement the model?

     d. Do any characteristics of the schools limit the ap-
plicability of the model?

C. General

   1. To what extent does the model have general applicability at schools with different characteristics from those
of Brunther College?

   2. Is the model a viable method of evaluating long-range
plans in private higher education?

   3. What areas for further research can be pursued to ex-
tend the usefulness of this study?

The original research addressed itself to each of these questions,
but not all of the findings are presented in this report, in the interest
of relevance and brevity.

Scope of the Study

Private schools, as opposed to state-supported institutions, were
chosen as the focus of this study since they depend more upon revenue from voluntary sources and a measure of financial feasibility
would be more meaningful to them. This factor, plus the physical
limitations of the study, made it desirable to restrict the research
to private higher education.

The number of private institutions is compared with the number
of state-supported colleges and universities in Table I.1. In the
seven years from 1962 to 1969 the percentage of private institutions
to total schools declined from 65 percent to 58 percent while the
percentage of private enrollments declined from 38.3 percent to
26.3 percent. In spite of this declining share of enrollment, private
education is still of substantial size and the absolute number of

TABLE I.1. Private and state-supported institutions of higher education, fall 1969 and fall 1962

	1969				1962			
	No. of schools	%	Enrollment	%	No. of schools	%	Enrollment	%
Private								
Two-year schools	252	10.0	127,372	1.6	213	10.0	71,341	.2
Four-year schools and universities	1,213	48.0	1,968,742	24.7	1,099	55.0	1,538,427	38.1
Total	1,465	58.0	2,096,114	26.3	1,312[a]	65.0	1,609,768	38.3
State-supported								
Two-year schools	634	25.1	1,819,509	22.8	351	17.0	520,987	12.4
Four-year schools	426	16.9	4,062,785	50.9	380	19.0	2,075,917	49.3
Total[b]	1,060	42.0	5,882,294	73.7	731	35.0	2,596,904	61.7
Total	2,525	100.0	7,978,408	100.0	2,043	100.0	4,206,672	100.0

Source: U.S. Office of Education, *Opening Fall Enrollment in Higher Education, 1969 and 1962* (Washington, D.C.: Govt. Printing Office, 1969 and 1962).

[a] In 1962–63, there were 817 private schools with some form of church association, according to a study sponsored by the Danforth Foundation (Manning M. Patillo, Jr., and Donald M. Mackenzie, *Church-sponsored Higher Education in the United States* [Washington, D.C.: American Council of Education, 1966]).

[b] Approximately 50 technical schools that offered no type of transfer credit are not included in the 1962 figures but are included in 1969.

schools and enrollment in fact increased, but most important, some of our schools of highest quality are privately supported.

Although the focus of this book is on private institutions, the concepts can also be applied in state institutions. Objectives in state schools may be more diverse than is typical in smaller private institutions, but many large private universities have programs of a magnitude that is clearly comparable with larger state universities. Further, as the description of the model is developed it will become apparent that one has only to recognize state financial support as another element in nontuition income calculations and the model immediately becomes applicable. The pertinent question is whether state universities have the necessary degree of centralization within the organization to make use of a model that emphasizes top administrative leadership.

Parameters around private higher education cannot be drawn with precision. In the past it may have been sufficient to draw a distinction between private and public institutions based on the source of revenue, but today almost all institutions receive public money in some form. The term *private* is frequently used as a synonym for *independent*, in reference to certain colleges. However, most private schools are not independent since a majority have some form of church association.

Several points do distinguish private institutions from state-supported (public) colleges and universities. From a budgetary point of view, both determine revenue by projecting income from endowments, gifts and grants, and other outside sources. Beyond this, state institutions have two additional sources of income: the tuition charged to students and the budget request to the state. But private colleges and universities can look only to tuition. Furthermore, the private school must set its tuition rates in competition with other schools, private as well as state-supported. In public institutions there is a prevailing opinion that capital additions which cannot be supported with federal grants should be financed with state funds. In private institutions capital additions not financed by federal funds must be financed by private donors or lenders.[5]

A final difference between the two concerns the authority and responsibility of their governing bodies. In state institutions that group receives its authority from the state and is responsible to the state for the efficient operation of the institution. In private schools the authority of the governing body comes from the charter or bylaws

[5] American Council on Education, *College and University Business Administration*, rev. ed. (Washington, D.C., 1968), p. 180; also, informal conversations with various administrators.

of the institution itself. Often this authority is stated in general terms to indicate the minimum expectation, and only custom or practice shapes the actual authoritative relationships with the group to whom the governing body is accountable. Neither is there a body of owners to hold the trustees accountable, except in those schools that are owned and operated directly by a religious organization.

Church association does not necessarily require that trustees account to the church, however. Manning M. Pattillo, Jr., and Donald M. Mackenzie conducted an extensive study of the church association of private colleges and universities for the Danforth Foundation. They found 817 institutions of higher education professing church relationships of one or more of the characteristics in Table I.2.

Throughout this study the terms *college* and *university* will be used, but again no clear distinction between the two concepts can be offered. In fact, there seems to be additional categories emerging,

TABLE I.2. Relationships of higher education institutions to sponsoring churches

Element of relationship	Frequency No.	%
1. Composition of board of control	687	84.1
a. Church membership required	574	70.3
b. Board members nominated/elected by church	438	53.6
2. Institution owned by church (or religious order or congregation)	573	70.1
3. Institution receives financial support from official church sources	766	93.7
a. For educational and general budget	602	73.7
b. In form of contributed services (Roman Catholic)	242	29.6
c. For capital purposes	364	44.6
4. Institution affiliated with church college organization/ subscribes to set of standards	631	77.2
a. Institution affiliated with denominational organization of colleges	529	64.7
b. Institution subscribes to standards or policy set by church for colleges	393	48.1
5. Institutional statement of purpose reflects religious orientation	782	95.7
6. Preference given church members in faculty and staff selection	575	70.4

Source: Manning M. Pattillo, Jr., and Donald M. Mackenzie, *Church-sponsored Higher Education in the United States* (Washington, D.C.: American Council on Education, 1966), chap. 3.
Note: A total of 817 church-related institutions were identified.

e.g., Clark Kerr's "multiversity."[6] There is also a noticeable trend among smaller colleges to expand their efforts into graduate education and into contract research. These schools seem to be in a fourth category between a college and a university, an institution that one might call a "miniversity." With this new group of institutions, colleges and universities might be classified as:

1. College: an institution of higher learning that emphasizes undergraduate teaching, with research or public service projects conducted by individual faculty members rather than by the institution itself.

2. Miniversity: an institution that emphasizes undergraduate teaching foremost but also offers graduate professional education (at the master's level), usually to meet specific or local demand. This school might also be involved in some research and public service projects but on a relatively small localized basis.

3. University: an institution that offers undergraduate education and several kinds of graduate professional education, probably including doctoral work. There would also be a functioning research organization involving faculty. Local public service projects may or may not be undertaken depending on the geographical location of the institution. National public service functions would probably involve the institution and a significant number of faculty.

4. Multiversity: this institution would be the higher education "supermarket" identified by Clark Kerr. It places considerable emphasis on graduate teaching, although there is also a large undergraduate program, on research, and on public service. This concept of higher education requires the massive allocation of resources that only a very few can afford. It carries with it the necessity for federal funds of a continuing nature and in large amounts. The prime example of this type of institution is the university system in California.

The private higher education institutions selected for the original research for this study ranged from a unitary college of about 1,100 undergraduates to a multiunit university of about 9,000 students at the undergraduate, masters, and doctoral level. They ranged from 65 years to 150 years in age. Their sources of income included one school that derived 85 percent of its income from tuition, room, and board and, at the other extreme, an institution where only 21 per-

[6] Clark Kerr, *The Uses of the University* (New York: Harper and Row, 1963), chap. 1.

cent of the income came from students. The church relationships were of the various types identified by Pattillo and Mackenzie; also included was one school with no church affiliation. The level of sophistication in long-range planning varied from that at one miniversity where the only planning was the annual budget submitted to the governing board to that at a university where long-range planning had been a continuing process for over ten years. All the institutions were accredited by regional agencies, and in addition several had professional accreditation of separate schools.

CHAPTER II

The Decision-making Environment in Private Higher Education

FINANCIAL planning should be viewed as one of the two phases in the management process—a planning stage, for the formulation of strategies and allocation of resources, and an implementation stage, for the direction and evaluation of organizational performance. The value of the model to be introduced here depends upon an understanding of the assumptions about the entire system. Since the model itself is drawn from concepts in business management, the process of which it is a part will also be discussed by comparing business and higher education. Certainly not all business practices are applicable to nonprofit colleges and universities, but some can be helpful and should be considered by higher education administrators.

Although long-term expenditures in higher education are not identical with capital expenditures in industry, the techniques of capital expenditure management provide a useful contrast to the process in private colleges. To illustrate this comparison consider the following outline as the analytical instrument.

I. Company policy (formulation)
   A. Statement of financial objectives
   B. Comparison of guidelines for evaluation of proposals
   C. Identification of the organizational structure
II. Company procedure (implementation)
   A. Initiation of project proposals
   B. Initial screening of proposals
   C. Analysis of the risk involved in the project
   D. Selection of the most advantageous proposals
   E. Approval of projects
   F. Appropriation of funds to specific projects

The procedural aspect (II) of implementing company policy will not be considered here since this study is concerned only with strategic financial planning, the policy formulation stage.

The major contributions of business to long-range financial planning and control have been in the three stages of company policy formulation for capital expenditure management. Basically, business has (1) refined the techniques of converting abstract missions into viable strategies, each of which is an "action plan" to accomplish some element of the total mission, (2) developed sophisticated quantitative measures of past and expected performance, and (3) identified effective organizational structures for people, financial resources, and physical facilities.

Statement of Financial Objectives (Policies)

1. For Capital Expenditures in Business

Corporate financial objectives for capital expenditures are concerned with the lifeblood of the business since it is these profit-producing investments that provide for survival and future growth. Generally, most statements of corporate objectives for capital investments consider a minimum acceptable rate of return, an acknowledgment of varying risk-classes, a level of protection for debt holders through restrictions on the amount of borrowed capital, and an indication of the financial obligation to the stockholders. These objectives taken from the "Frontier Rubber Company Case" are representative:

1. To increase earnings per share
2. To maintain a dividend pay-out of approximately 65 percent
3. To maintain a long-term debt ratio of 35 percent or less of capitalization (in this company capitalization referred to as long-term debt plus equity)[1]

There are degrees of difference among the financial objectives of companies, but all are concerned with increasing the economic well-being of the stockholders without jeopardizing the firm's solvency. Even though some writers view solvency as a supporting function to profitability, the two cannot be completely separated since long-term profitability depends upon solvency.

A stockholder's economic interest in a particular common stock investment centers on dividend receipts and growth in market value. Recognizing this, many companies include in their capital expenditure objectives a statement of a desired dividend pay-out ratio, intended to support the stockholder's desire for a cash return as well as to stimulate an increase in the market value of the shares. In addition, the dividend pay-out ratio assures the firm

---

[1] "Frontier Rubber Company," ICH 4F68R, prepared by Joseph L. Fromm, under the direction of Robert F. Vandell, Harvard Graduate School of Business Administration, 1959, p. 2.

that sufficient funds will remain to provide for internal growth and to maintain solvency.

Each project proposed through a capital investment system is evaluated in terms of its contribution to the stated objectives. In addition to profitability and solvency, projects must meet the test of such other criteria as an optimum level of risk of failure for the project or to the firm, compatibility with the firm's type of business, and desirability in terms of social responsibility. These factors frequently cannot be measured in quantitative terms, as is also the case with most academic objectives.

In industry many capital expenditures are made for reasons other than profitability. For instance, there is no direct profit expected from air and water pollution equipment, from air-conditioning the office, or from carpeting and decorating the executive offices. Quite naturally, no attempt is made to measure these expenditures in terms of a rate of ROI.

The financial objectives of a business and those of colleges and universities differ mainly in the fact that the nonprofit institutions do not have stockholders with profitability expectations and usually do not make capital investments for the purpose of producing a profit. This lack of a profit objective is a fundamental characteristic of the higher education institutions.

2. For Long-Term Expenditures in Higher Education

When one views the vast array of programs underway in the 2,600 institutions of higher learning in the United States, it is difficult to detect a coherent objective applicable to all. What is more alarming, the difficulty is only slightly diminished when one examines any given school. The whole concept of purpose seems to have been ignored in an environment in which learning of almost any kind could attract a crowd. In the last twenty-five years education has been an easy product to sell. Too many schools have been concerned solely with growth for the sake of size, with little attention to the direction of the growth. But in the past two or three years the environment has changed stringently, especially for private institutions. Financial health is now of vital importance, so much so that it may be an overriding objective in a majority of private and state schools.[2] The financial objective for private colleges and universities, in generalized terms, is to offer to its segment of the public a particular selection of academic programs that are within the

[2] *Chronicle of Higher Education,* Dec. 7, 1970, p. 1.

financial feasibility of the institution. This objective was implicit or explicit in the programs of the institutions participating in this study.

Generally, all the schools expected auxiliary enterprises to be self-supporting and, if possible, to make a contribution to the operating fund or, to put it another way, to have cash revenue in excess of cash expenses (including debt service). Broadly speaking, the latter might be construed as a profit-making function. Profit, as the term is used in industry, refers to the excess of revenue received or accrued over all expenses paid or incurred. It is the amount available to purchase assets or to pay dividends to owners. The financial objectives for the auxiliary enterprises are somewhat similar to the profit function in industry, but the preponderance of expenditures in higher education correspond to those business capital expenditures which are not expected to provide a profit and therefore must be evaluated by other criteria. Expenditures for auxiliary enterprises are considered and included in evaluation by the model presented here, although profitability measures could be developed to evaluate them instead.

Academic programs and projects, the primary interest of this study, were obviously not looked upon as income-producing. Rather, each individual proposal was evaluated first for academic value and then for the economic ability of the institution to support it. The relative emphasis placed on academic values as opposed to financial considerations can be seen in the philosophies of several of the institutions. The large university expected funds for the construction of academic buildings to be on hand before the project was started. At two of the smaller schools where a high proportion of the income came from student fees, all new academic programs were to be either self-supporting or replacements of existing programs.

A notable exception to the conservative approach of these schools was observed at the miniversity that had the highest proportion of student income. There the need to upgrade the college was believed to be more important than financial considerations, and as a result, financial objectives were secondary to academic purposes. No explicit financial objective could be observed, but the implicit purpose seemed to be to let the financial need in the future serve to attract the required funds. Substantial capital additions were needed to implement the new programs, and commitments were made even though a severe strain on finances would occur in the next few years. The financial difficulty could also be traced to gifts and grants that were designated for specific projects, such as a new building, when there was no source of funds for continued operation of the building other than the operating budget. Finally, excessive use of debt added substantially to the operating budgets for the next few years. Because of this long-range financial strain other institutions have taken the position that buildings will not be started until the source of operating funds is known.

It has been pointed out previously that financial objectives in business usually limit the debt level of the firm through the ratio of liquid assets to currently maturing liabilities, as well as through a desired ratio of debt to total assets or to stockholder's equity. In addition, there are acceptable ratios of interest on debt to the firm's earnings before interest, which are intended to serve as a guideline measurement of the effect on profitability. These ratios are not sufficient to determine the debt capacity in private colleges and universities. As the financial vice-president of one of the miniversities pointed out, there is no profit with which to compare the interest charges. Even more frustration in the use of business guidelines is caused by the lack of legal capital. There are only "fund balances," which have no legal limitations to protect debtors other than those imposed by donors of endowment funds. Even the traditional methods of accounting in colleges and universities deter the use of debt level ratios taken from business. This is not a criticism of the fund-accounting techniques; rather, it is an explanation of the lack of applicability of certain business measurements.

In a business, debtors view the ratio of total debt to owner's equity as a test of the strength of their position in case of liquidation of the firm. Fund balances in private colleges and universities do not provide a similar cushion; consequently the debt-to-equity ratio is not valid. There is even a question of what the liquidation value of a college might be. Even a small school may have assets valued at several million dollars, and interested buyers with this amount of money are few in number. The most ready market for defunct private colleges has been the state systems and, infrequently, larger private institutions. In many ways the combination has resembled a pooling of interest between businesses. The assets and liabilities of the two are combined as of a given date; the larger institution survives and assumes the debts of the smaller school.

The schools under study were using several rules of thumb about the use of debt. Only one school used debt for academic building; the other four restricted its use to self-liquidating projects such as dormitories and student centers. Additionally, total debt was limited to the size of the endowment fund in some instances where the fund was relatively small. The position seemed to emerge as a matter of the ability to meet principal and interest payments without creating pressure on the operating budget requiring higher enrollment.

Use of debt at the various schools can be observed in Table II.1.

TABLE II.1. Assets and debt at the five institutions

	Assets	Debt	Debt/assets
Small college	$ 14.0 mil.	$3.0 mil.	21.4%
Miniversity B	23.4 mil.	6.3 mil.	27.0%
Well-endowed college	32.0 mil.	1.0 mil.	3.1%
Large university	194.2 mil.	6.0 mil.	3.0%
Miniversity A (low endowment)	9.0 mil.	1.4 mil.	15.5%
Miniversity A 3 years later	16.5 mil.	6.5 mil.	39.3%

An analysis of the sources of income at these five schools can provide further insight into the divergent views on debt use. Some interesting relationships can be observed in Table II.2 between

TABLE II.2. Sources of income and debt levels at the five institutions

	Total income[a]	Nontuition income	Col. 2/ col. 1	Debt/assets
Small college	$ 2,272,000	$ 432,000	19.0%	21.4%
Miniversity B	3,877,000	1,212,000[b]	31.3	27.0
Well-endowed college	3,904,000	1,643,000	42.0	3.1
Large university	25,421,000	14,400,000[c]	56.6	3.0
Miniversity A (low endowment)	2,283,000	336,000	14.7	15.5
Miniversity A 3 years later	3,918,000	1,538,000	39.3	39.3

[a] Income includes the net excess of revenue over expenses of auxiliary enterprises.

[b] Miniversity B's nontuition income from gifts and grants had only recently increased to the level indicated by the figures for 1967.

[c] Research revenue has been eliminated since it was used to pay research expenses approximately equal to the total revenue received for this purpose.

debt levels and the amount of nontuition income. At the better-endowed schools much larger proportions of the total income were derived from nontuition sources, and only about 3 percent of the assets was financed by debt. Other schools with lower endowments made greater use of debt to finance expanding and anticipated innovation programs. This analysis raises the question of the extent to which policies on financing of long-term expenditures are dictated by expedience as opposed to planning. Would the "no debt" policy on academic programs at the well-endowed institutions stand if their sources of outside income were cut off or diminished? Should the others limit their growth to that which can be financed from non-tuition income? These questions are intermingled with the broader concern of private schools not to diminish the quality of the educational program. When do financial constraints become crucial? Certainly it is better to face this issue in advance, in the planning process, not at the actual moment of crisis when options are seriously limited. The proposed model is expected to provide helpful information to administrators in the planning process, even if it only tells them how many years they have left.

In business, profit is expected eventually to repay long-term projects that are financed with debt (assuming no additional investment is made by the owners). If one looks beyond the accounting methods in business and in higher education, it becomes apparent that in both instances debt is repaid from operating income. In this sense, this leads to the conclusion that when debt is used the final limit should be measured in terms of the ability to repay it. The prevailing opinion of administrators was that, with tuition rates (the major source of income) already considerably in excess of the rates in state institutions, little room was left to add debt service as another operating expenditure from current funds. The model proposed in this study will be helpful in evaluating the feasibility of debt repayment; nevertheless, the whole concept of the use of debt by private colleges needs further research.

Comparison of Guidelines for Evaluation of Proposals

1. For Capital Expenditures in Business

In addition to viable objectives for capital expenditures, businesses have to set a policy on the types of investments to make and the methods to use in measuring the return. Businesses have been measuring ROI for many years, on both past and expected performance. The degree of sophistication has been increasing rapidly, particularly in the last ten to fifteen years; yet business still does not have the one best method. Companies use the pay-back, the unadjusted ROI, the discounted cash-flow, or the net present value to evaluate capital expenditures, as well as variations of all these methods.[3] Regardless of the method a company selects, the intention is to relate the project's annual profit expected from the capital expenditure over a period of time to the required investment.[4] The ultimate evaluation, then, is the rate of ROI.

Because of its crucial nature, the ROI measurement often overshadows other evaluations required in making capital expenditure decisions. Analyses must be made of functional aspects of investments for new machinery, production capability for new plants, and many other matters. But all are aimed at determining the utility of the projects and at refining estimates of ROI. The motivating objective of profit expectations also has to be evaluated. It is with these profits that the firm achieves its growth, replaces its assets at constantly increasing prices, and rewards the owners. It is the financial objective that is of concern here.

In order to make a decision on a specific capital expenditure, managers at various levels need the following information:

1. Funds to be committed to the project
2. Expected return (s) from the investment
3. Length of life of the project, of the flow of returns, or of both
4. Estimate of the degree of risk in the project
5. Measure of this project's returns in comparison with other available alternatives
6. Other noneconomic factors favorable and unfavorable to the project
7. Available funds for this and all other projects
8. Understanding of the company capital expenditure objectives[5]

Both in the literature on capital budgeting and in the cases analyzed, the amount of attention given to these factors varied

[3] Most business finance textbooks dealing with capital budgeting discuss these various methods. A comprehensive comparison can be examined in National Association of Accountants, *Financial Analysis to Guide Capital Expenditure Decisions*, Research Report no. 43 (New York, 1967), chap. 3.

[4] A number of companies now use methods of measuring ROI that adjust both expenditures and revenue to reflect the fact that future expenditures and revenue have a different value to the firm from dollars spent or earned currently. This results from the fact that dollars on hand now can be invested profitably and produce more dollars. This adjustment is caused by the time-value of money, which is not a major consideration in colleges and universities except possibly for the evaluation of endowment funds. Although private colleges and universities may have a need for revenue in excess of expenses (in the industrial accounting sense), this is not the motivating objective. Consequently, adjustments for the earning value of money do not seem appropriate.

[5] Robert W. Johnson, *Financial Management*, 3rd ed. (Boston: Allyn and Bacon, 1966), chap. 8.

and other types of needed information were mentioned. However, this list points to the kind of policy needed for an effective system of evaluating capital expenditures.

In recent years considerable attention has been given to guidelines for the evaluation of risk in capital expenditure proposals. The uncertainty in proposals is viewed as affecting the degree of risk of failure of the project as well as the degree of risk to the firm itself. The common stockholder looks at the risk in capital investments in terms of the effect the project failure (and degrees thereof) would have on earnings per share, on dividends per share, or on market value. Companies approach this part of the analysis in various ways, but a method referred to in the "Consolidated Electrical Products Case" is not uncommon (Table II.3). Generally,

TABLE II.3. Risk classification at Consolidated Electrical Products Company

	Degree of risk		
Category of project	Normal	Moderate	High
Cost reduction or replacement	Min. std. rate	Normal plus?	Moderate plus?
Plant expansion	Min. std. plus 5%	Normal plus?	Moderate plus?
Major process innovation or new products	Min. std. plus 10%	Normal plus?	Moderate plus?
Necessary projects	Subjective	— —	— —

Source: Robert F. Vandell, "Consolidated Electric Products, Inc." (A) through (E), ICH 4F78, Harvard College, 1958–59.

a matrix approach is used to classify projects into four categories and within each to determine (perhaps subjectively) whether the risk is normal, moderate, or high for each category. A company then would require a higher ROI within each category as the degree of risk increased, although CONELP handled this quite loosely. All the methods for refinement of risk in measuring ROI are based ultimately on judgment. In the CONELP matrix judgment is required to determine normal, moderate, or high risk. It is not known whether the measurement of risk is a widely used procedure; at this point, much of the consideration of this element seems to be confined to the finance literature.[6]

[6] David B. Hertz, "Risk Analysis in Capital Investments," *Harvard Business Review,* Jan.–Feb. 1964, reprinted in *Capital Investment Decisions,* reprint series

2. *For Strategic Expenditures in Private Colleges and Universities*

Obviously, no quantitative measure corresponding to a rate of ROI was found in the policies of the five participating schools. On the other hand, schools have adopted other policies as a result of previous deficits in the operating funds. Two schools, as stated previously, were operating under the policy that all new academic programs would have to be either replacements for existing programs or capable of generating their own financial support. This guideline had developed from a crisis situation and supposedly was not intended to be a continuing policy. The large university policy of requiring that funds be on hand or explicitly identified for new academic buildings was of a more permanent nature and apparently was understood by all administrators and academic department chairmen. Four of five institutions also expected auxiliary enterprises to support themselves, including the repayment of debt incurred to finance the enterprise, but even here rates of ROI were not used as a measurement.

No clear guideline concerning debt capacity was found. Although the more affluent schools restricted debt to self-liquidating projects such as dormitories, it was not certain whether they would retain this policy if growth was restricted. At the other schools debt was used but with no clear understanding among administrators about its ultimate level. Despite the concern about excessive debt, and a general feeling that there was a ceiling, no guidelines had been spelled out for guidance in the planning process.

The risks to private education had been discussed in the press at great length, and the comments of all administrators showed an awareness of the dangers.[7] For the private colleges, debt may seem at first glance an enticing method of financing growth and innovation or merely of keeping pace with state-supported schools. The danger lies in the inability to keep tuition rates low enough to attract the necessary number of students. Table I.1 indicates that the student market available for private schools has not risen as fast as the number of private institutions. This means greater competition for students in order to meet increasing budgets. The

---

of HBR; Harry Markowitz, *Portfolio Selection,* monograph for Cowles Foundation for Research in Economics, Yale University (New York: John Wiley & Sons, 1959) ; Ralph O. Swalm, "Utility Theory—Insights into Risk Taking," *Harvard Business Review,* Nov.–Dec. 1966, pp. 123–135.

[7] *Business Week,* Sept. 21, 1969; c.f. *Fortune,* Feb. 1967; *Chronicle of Higher Education,* various issues.

solution all too often is to lower admission standards, which eventually will dispel the public's image of the quality education they offer and put the private schools into direct competition with state-supported schools. Under these conditions the debt that must be repaid from operating income may become a burden. The availability of federal loans at low interest rates or federal subsidies would not appreciably alter the situation. With a high proportion of costs committed and ever-increasing, debt repayment could be the expenditure that pushes a private school over the brink.

Even though the five participating schools had not developed explicit policies, these financial risks were apparent:

1. Rapid expansion of programs could exceed the ability to finance them.
2. Sources of gifts and grants would not increase as fast as the increase in operating costs.
3. Competition from state-supported institutions, particularly the two-year community colleges, may tend to reduce enrollment or at least reduce the pool of applicants.
4. Public interest in private higher education may diminish because of either the changing values in society or a decline in the quality of education resulting from the competitive conditions in 3.

Identification of Organization and Information Systems

1. For Capital Expenditure Management in Business

An efficient system for managing capital expenditures requires a policy statement identifying organizational lines of authority and responsibility. The "International Harvester Company Case" illustrates one company's organization for managing capital expenditures.[8] Its process was in "two distinct preliminary stages; compilation of the capital budget and the actual appropriation of funds." In the budgeting stage, managers at lower levels were expected to identify projects that they wished to submit for funding over various periods of time. The budgets went up through channels of a conventional pyramid organization to a "finance group," through the controller for capital budgets, the corporate operations

---

[8] Robert N. Anthony, John Dearden, and Richard F. Vancil, *Management Control Systems* (Homewood, Ill.: Richard D. Irwin, 1965), pp. 493–506.

review committee, and to the board of directors. These approved budgets became the source of financial planning at the corporate level.

The approved budgets were not authorization for expenditures. This was obtained in the second stage by routing an expenditure request through approximately the same channels. Approval of the request constituted the appropriation of funds. As a follow-up on the system, International Harvester operated a loose, postcompletion audit procedure. Procedures for budgeting and appropriation were spelled out in a "Capital Expenditures Policies and Procedures Manual."

Developing a formal organization to process capital expenditures does not accomplish the purpose of getting people at various positions in the company involved in the management of these capital investments. People have to be assigned to the "slots" in the organization, and their roles must be spelled out. In larger corporations, this assignment is a policy matter involving position descriptions that include statements specifying individual's roles in the system of managing capital expenditures.

Operating managers such as division managers, production managers, or sales managers are given, as part of their duties, responsibility in the capital budgeting process. These people are relied upon for many of the ideas for cost-saving investments, new products, new production processes, new sales offices, and for much of the innovation necessary for a successful firm.[9] They usually initiate the request for a large portion of the capital budget and make the initial estimates of return on investment.

At other levels in the organization, staff engineers and accountants check proposals from operating personnel and compile the proposals into a budget for the corporation. This budget often is scrutinized by committees and revised as necessary. The chief operating officer usually has final approval of the budget that is to be submitted to the board of directors. The method of financing generally is determined at the corporate level before submission to the directors. The "International Harvester Company Case" offers a comprehensive policy in this area and generally illustrates the various responsibilities at each level.[10]

[9] Robert F. Vandell, "Note on the Capital Allocation Process," UVA-F-121, Sponsors of the Graduate School of Business Administration, University of Virginia, 1966, p. 4.

[10] Anthony, Dearden, and Vancil.

2. *For Strategic Expenditure Administration in Private Colleges*

In contrast to the reasonably clear lines of responsibility and authority in business, the organizational structure in higher education is diffused between faculty and administration with the trustees as a possible third distinctive group of decision makers. (In recent months the role of students has also been under discussion as a fourth possible entrant into the decision-making process.) Final authority over all facets of an institution's program rests in the governing board, but current practices have confused the decision-making process to such a degree that it is more helpful to discuss three centers of responsibility and authority.

Formal organization charts for each of the five institutions are exhibited at the end of this chapter (Exhibits II.1–5). There is wide disagreement as to who the decision makers are in higher education, and it is doubtful that the charts tell an accurate story about responsibility and authority in all policy areas. The two major policy areas under dispute are educational policy (academic affairs) and financial affairs (including asset management). To some degree responsibility and authority in these two areas is claimed by trustees, by the president (administration), and by the faculty, with students now also complicating the issue.

The President. The role of the college president has evolved as has the institution itself. Most early presidents of the colleges were drawn from the clergy because they were the learned men of the day and because the schools were founded partly in order to educate ministers. In the latter part of the nineteenth century, as the institutions became larger and more diverse in purpose and organization, these presidents from the clergy were considered inadequate to the task of administering the sprawling universities. They were criticized, not for intellectual ineptitude, but for their inability to cope with the complexities of managing people, raising funds, dealing with politicians, disciplining students, and all the other tasks that confronted the college president.[11]

At the beginning of the twentieth century, Frederick Rudolph has said,

Actually the college and university president was on the way to being someone . . . whose remoteness from the students would be paralleled by his remoteness from learning itself.

[11] Frederick Rudolph, *The American College and University* (New York: Alfred A. Knopf, 1965), chap. 1.

The office increasingly . . . called for a . . . manager who could perform for higher education those functions which elsewhere in American society were being performed by the captains of industry and the captains of finance.[12]

At this time,

The clergyman president went into discard because he lacked skill in the ways of administration, because his commitment to the classical curriculum stood in the way of the more practical and popular emphasis which commended itself to the trustees, and because the world in which the colleges and universities now moved was more secular, less subject to religious influences.[13]

So the status of the clergy in the president's office diminished as the colleges and universities entered the twentieth century. The universities themselves, with their size and complexity, created a need for administrators; during the period 1890–1925 the transition was particularly noticeable.

John J. Corson has pointed out that the college president shares the opportunity and the authority of decision-making.[14] He shares with the faculty the opportunity to make decisions regarding the educational programs, *"if they allow him to participate."* Corson also points to the "fixed" nature of the faculty salaries, which prevents the president from using the budget to influence materially the course of education; he can influence only additions to the program. He shares with the trustees those responsibilities which they delegate to him. In larger institutions he shares responsibilities with alumni for such things as athletics and fund-raising programs.

Corson predicted that in the future some presidents, if not all of them, will not be able to function as educators at all and that it would be futile for them to try. Their role will be that of administrators of educational programs in an educational institution, but the president himself seems to be evolving to a role outside the educational purposes of the institution he administers. Few boards and presidents are as dogmatic as they are empowered to be by the charter and bylaws of the institution.[15] In many cases they condone or allow faculty practices that are not contributing to efficient

---

[12] *Ibid.*, p. 418.

[13] *Ibid.*, p. 419.

[14] Corson, "Roles and Responsibilities in Management in IHL," in *Challenge and Change in American Education*, ed. Seymour E. Harris, Kenneth M. Deitch, and Alan Levensohn (Berkeley, Calif.: McCutchan, 1965), pp. 235–37.

[15] Mary Woods Bennett, "Changes within Liberal Arts Colleges," in *Emerging Patterns in American Higher Education*, ed. Logan Wilson (Washington, D.C.: American Council on Education, 1965), p. 64.

operations. None of the presidents at the five institutions in this study felt that they had the authority to install educational policy without faculty agreement, although several did see a role for themselves in initiating new ideas and promoting them through faculty committees or through academic departments. None felt that they had the authority to give final approval to major changes in the academic programs; rather, they believed that they should carry their recommendations to the board of trustees. At the large university a faculty group had initiated a proposal for a separate Graduate School of Business Administration, a faculty committee had discussed and approved it, and the president had recommended it to the board of trustees. At miniversity B the president had conceived the International Studies Program, suggested it to the faculty, and carried it to the trustees for final approval. At miniversity A the president's office and interested faculty groups had jointly recommended a new Graduate Division; a faculty committee had discussed the proposal, and the president had recommended it to the trustees. Additions and deletions of courses in each of the schools seldom were brought to the attention of the trustees or even the president unless special financial considerations were involved.

The president's control over financial matters is now recognized to be limited by tenured appointments of faculty members. Once tenure is offered, there are fewer options available to the president in the preparation of the annual budget, which in part explains the opinion offered by several college presidents that giving tenure to a professor is one of the most expensive decisions facing college administrators.

There was little question that each of the presidents had the responsibility to propose the annual operating budget, capital budget, and related financial projections, that it was the trustees' responsibility to approve the budget, but that its implementation rested with the president and his designated administrators. The trustees also generally delegated control over expenditures during the year to the president and from him to others in the administration. Financial policies implemented through this structure eventually are confronted by the academic needs of the institution, expressed through the faculty organization.

A major responsibility of the president is to resolve, or at least minimize, this conflict between trustees and faculty. He cannot administer his office with the same degree of authoritative power as the corporation president does, though he occupies a similar position on the organization chart. His importance is not derived from an authoritarian position but from his role as an innovator, a coordinator, a molder of attitudes and objectives, and a caretaker of resources. He may also be a fund-raiser and serve as the public's image of the institution.

One authoritative document, the "Statement on Government of Colleges and Universities" issued by the American Association of University Professors (AAUP), the American Council on Education, and the Association of Governing Boards of Universities and Colleges, has spelled out the president's role in the long-range planning process: "As the chief planning officer of an institution, the president has a special obligation to innovate and initiate. The degree to which a president can envision new horizons for his institution, and can persuade others to see them and to work toward them, will often constitute the chief measure of his administration.[16] Because of this role, much of the initiative for strategic changes originate in the president's office, and for this reason, the financial planning model proposed here can best be utilized by the president and his top administrators.

The Trustees. The trustees represent still another center of authority and responsibility in an institution of higher learning. In the early institutions, many of the trustees were also clergymen. Ministers in the early days played a prominent role in the life of every community. They were looked to for many decisions and played many roles that were by today's standards somewhat remote from their status as clergymen. Interestingly enough, the trustee today is viewed as a policy-maker, and we now think of businessmen as having considerable competence in this area.[17]

The legal organization of trustees has evolved in one of two ways. The first is exemplified at Harvard, where the governing board itself is incorporated, this board constitutes the body of the corporation, and the assets of the corporation are held in the name of this incorporated body. The other approach has been to incorporate the institution with the governing board serving as the responsible agent.[18]

[16] Reprinted in the *Chronicle of Higher Education,* Jan. 1967; also reprinted as a teaching note by the University of Virginia Graduate School of Business Administration with permission of the *Chronicle of Higher Education,* UVA A&P-1, p. 5.

[17] Rudolph, p. 173.

[18] Gerald P. Burns, *Trustees in Higher Education* (New York: Independent College Fund of America, 1966), pp. 5–14.

William S. Paley, in his report on the role of the trustees at
Columbia University, identified several major legal responsibilities
of trustees:

1. To select and appoint the president of the university
2. To be finally responsible for the acquisition, conservation,
   and management of the university's funds and properties
3. To oversee and approve the kinds of education offered by the
   university and make certain that its quality meets the highest
   standards possible[19]

Another writer, Gerald P. Burns, quotes Ordway Tead concerning the role of the trustee. "Trustees are, of course, in the last
analysis, holding the operation of education *in trust as a public
service*. Every college has now become in fact a public agency; and
it is required to gain and hold public confidence."[20] In the private
institution the trustee must resolve the issue of his public responsibility, which may be opposed to the desires of faculty, administrators, students, the church sponsor, or other interested factions. Burns
refers to the power of the board as collective and democratic, not
executive, and as legislative.

When a group of trustees were asked whether or not they should
consider questions on admissions policy, ratio of faculty to students,
and so on, they answered that they considered these specialized
matters and solely the problems of the faculty and dean. They felt
no obligation as trustees to consider them.[21] The "Statement on
Government of Colleges and Universities" declared: "The governing board of an institution of higher education, while maintaining
a general overview, entrusts the conduct of administration to the
administrative officers, the president, and the deans, and the conduct
of teaching and research to the faculty. The board should undertake appropriate self-limitation."[22] Most writers agree that trustees
have final responsibility for the control and management of the
institution but that their role in educational policy is not so pre-
cisely defined. By custom they have remained aloof from educational
policy, relying on the faculty.

In addition, in private institutions it is not certain to whom the
trustees themselves are responsible, unless they are asked by a church

---

[19] *Ibid.*, p. 133.

[20] *Ibid.*, p. 12.

[21] Corson, in Harris, Deitch, and Levensohn, eds., p. 235. It should be noted
that on the small college campus the president is usually looked upon as chief
administrative officer as well as the chairman of the faculty but that his
academic role seems to be diminishing.

[22] UVA A&P-1, p. 5.

body to account for their action. Historically the denominations have not pressed for accountability and have tended to look upon their colleges as another agency demanding scarce church funds. In state institutions the governing board is responsible to the state government, either the governor or the state legislature. This accountability is, in fact, an operating responsibility with specific policies on the kinds of control and responsibility that are expected of the governing board. In the private institution there is no similar body to whom the trustees are responsible. They are responsible in a legal sense to the state for the conduct of the institution as set forth in the charter under which it was incorporated. But beyond this minimal responsibility, usually worded in general terms, there is nothing to specify a competent higher authority.

When one adds to this lack of higher authority the fact that there is no measure of efficiency or effectiveness available to the trustee in evaluating the institution, the dilemma is obvious. It is little wonder that boards of trustees become advisory boards and presidents get board action through consensus opinion even though formal votes are registered.[23] This method of operation may continue until a crisis situation arises which forces trustees to become involved. It has become traditional that a rejection of a president's request on a major issue is construed as a "no confidence" vote, frequently leading to a president's resignation. Under these conditions, a president is well advised to keep in contact with the mood and inclination of his board through committees and other informal methods.

On the other hand, an effective president is often able to sway individual board members, particularly since the president probably recommended the trustee's appointment. This gives the president de facto authority and makes him responsible for the conduct of the institution. Only some act that diametrically opposes the broad purposes of an educational institution or that arouses public disfavor would cause a college president to find difficulty with his board.

At the five participating institutions the role of trustees was much the same as stated in the literature. In the area of financial affairs, the trustees were the final authority, but they looked to the president and his staff for operational support as well as for innovative ideas. Educational policy concerned them only when it was involved in the total operation of the school and when major changes in pro-

---

[23] Burns, p. 12.

gram were contemplated. Within these broad parameters, educational policy had been effectively delegated to the faculty.

The Faculty. The decision-making process in higher education is diffused in a third direction by the faculty role. The attitude toward faculty involvement in administrative matters varies from school to school, with several factors contributing to the degree of involvement. In some schools faculty members have academic freedom, tenure, respect of their colleagues, respect of the community in which they live, and professional recognition within their discipline, all of which make it at least desirable for administrators to seek their opinion on educational policy matters whether or not there is any stated responsibility to ask for these judgments.[24]

In attempting to clarify the areas of authority and responsibility in small colleges, Beardsley Ruml relegated the role of the faculty to the lowest position in relation to the administration and trustees. Even in regard to curriculum and educational policy,

the liberal college faculty *as a body* is not competent to make the judgments and evaluations required to design a curriculum in liberal education. The individual members of the faculty are for the most part chosen as specialists in departmental subjects, and as a result both of knowledge and personal interest each is a special advocate, necessarily and desirably so. A collection of special advocates cannot be expected to be a repository and a voice of judicial wisdom. . . .

The trustees of a college choose unwisely when they refer the problem of curriculum for decision to the corporate faculty. They choose unwisely, and yet the responsibility for the curriculum still remains of necessity with the Trustees.[25]

Ruml further declared:

The Board of Trustees has in fact final responsibility under its charter for the educational program as well as for the property of its institution. Having final authority and responsibility, it also has accountability for a performance it is willing to defend to the state, to the national and local community, to donors of property, to parents and students, to the individual members of the faculty who have committed themselves and their families to an educational and intellectual program as their way of life.[26]

A contrasting opinion on the subject of faculty authority has been given by David Fellman, professor of political science at the

[24] Corson, in Harris, Deitch, and Levensohn, eds., pp. 235–37.

[25] Beardsley Ruml and Donald H. Morrison, *Memo to a College Trustee* (New York: McGraw-Hill, 1959) , p. 7.

[26] *Ibid.,* p. 13.

University of Wisconsin and former president of AAUP. He quoted from the AAUP 1915 Declaration of Principles: "although professors are the appointees of the university's trustees, they are not in any proper sense the trustees' employees, just as Federal judges are appointed by the President without becoming, as a consequence, his employees."[27] He also cited the AAUP *Bulletin* of June 1960, which says:

The basic functions of a college or university are to augment, preserve, criticize, and transmit knowledge and to foster creative capacities. . . . These functions are performed by a community of scholars who must be free to exercise independent judgment in the planning and execution of their educational responsibilities.[28]

Fellman stated that "although the language of the charters or the parent statutes implies that the boards are theoretically all-powerful, normally this is not descriptive of the realities in the educational world." The boards of trustees are usually too large and are forced to rubber-stamp committee recommendations; they have too few meetings to keep abreast of conditions and issues; they generally accept the recommendations of the president; and they are too deeply involved during their brief time in session with finances, property management, and public relations to demonstrate much concern over educational matters.[29]

Fellman gives more power to the faculty than most writers do, just as Ruml gives more weight to the governing board. The joint "Statement on Government of Colleges and Universities" made fewer general statements on faculty responsibility than on the responsibilities of the governing board and the administration. Instead, it identified specific areas of faculty responsibility—curriculum, methods of instruction, research, student life as it pertains to the educational process, degree requirements, faculty appointments, tenure, and dismissal. These areas had recognizable limits. "Budgets, manpower limitation, the time element, and the policies of other groups, bodies, and agencies having jurisdiction over the institution may set limits to realization of faculty advice.[30]

The academic freedom to which Fellman referred is relatively new.[31] Before about 1900 a professor's freedom was restricted to the right to teach his subject in the manner he saw fit, and only

---

[27] Fellman, "The Academic Community: Who Decides What?," in *Whose Goals for American Higher Education,* ed. Charles G. Dobbin and Calvin B. T. Lee (Washington, D.C.: American Council on Education, 1968), p. 108.

[28] *Ibid.,* p. 109.   [29] *Ibid.,* p. 114.   [30] UVA A&P-1, p. 6.

[31] Rudolph, pp. 410–16.

that. In colonial days, even the rights to publish and speak freely were restricted by the customs and opinions of the day as the institution interpreted them. Certainly no faculty member was allowed to say or do things that deterred or detracted from the mission of the institution. The teacher's professional standing did not generate from his teaching but from his position in law, medicine, or the clergy.

The range of matters in which teachers feel they have academic freedom has been expanding constantly, especially since the formation of the AAUP in 1915. The range is far smaller if viewed from the perspective of either the administration or the trustees. No universally accepted definition of academic freedom is available, although the 1940 Statement of Principles by the AAUP has been adopted as the official position of a large number of institutions as well as academic associations.

There was ample evidence at all five participating institutions of the awareness of the faculty's academic freedom, but there emphasis on various points differed. At the large university, one administrator was quite definite about the autonomy of the faculty: "Academic policy is entirely the responsibility of the faculty. . . . The trustees only get into academic decisions when major program changes are under consideration such as the School of Business Administration proposal and the School of Computer Science."

The president of the small college said positively:

This school is faculty-oriented. It is not a cleavage though. I think the faculty dimension is not a stronger dimension than the administrative dimension. There have been faculty people who were critical of the "Task Force" [a study of the changes proposed in degree requirements] which was not my idea. It really came out of the faculty. It is forcing them to do some thinking and they find it difficult. I tell them that if they don't want it, we will run the kind of school they do want.

At one of the miniversities the president was attempting to unite the school and did not see the clear lines of demarcation that other administrators suggest:

This is an objective, too, to become a university, not just four warring camps. I would say that it might be easier to divide and conquer the faculty in terms of specific objectives but there are other objectives including this strong spirit of unity which you really can't accomplish unless you move together.

At still another school, the president stated:

The faculty is a very strong force on this campus. I don't want to overstate this. I am not sure anything happens here without the faculty participating in it. The budget is actually adopted only after faculty needs are satisfied. No faculty committee consults about the budget but it's a strong indirect influence. The faculty is entrusted with the responsibility for deciding on all the educational goals and decisions. Of course, the Board of Trustees has final authority on everything.

It should be noted that department chairmen at the large university had considerably more financial information than those at the other schools. This information included data on the salaries of their faculty and general information about the total university budget. Although the department chairmen most likely considered the effect of a new course or program on the financial position of the university, this restraint was not required as part of any proposal they made to the curriculum committee. Financial responsibility at lower levels probably resulted from the university's larger size and organizational complexity, which required the delegation of responsibility and authority. To some extent, the department chairmen, or at least the deans of individual schools, had responsibility and authority comparable to those of the presidents of the smaller institutions.

The Students. Throughout the time this study was being made, the student movement increased significantly in momentum. The traditional three parties to decision-making in higher education have now been joined by a fourth—the students. The "free university" and its virtual control by students represents the most extreme degree of the involvement they are seeking, but this institution has had a relatively insignificant existence to date. However, there remains a demand by students for a high level of involvement in the governing of their institutions. Policy statements of the U.S. National Student Association (USNSA) illustrate this point quite clearly.[32] This organization of student governments seeks for its members to "be directly involved in academic policy making." They feel that "student government and the administration and trustees have a reciprocal duty to communicate before either makes basic policy decisions affecting the campus community. . . . In addition to the minimum right of prior discussions, student government should participate in the decisions upon basic policy." And finally, they want the student government to be "in active participation in the formulation of long-range policy for the college community." They stress the goals of mutual relationships and responsibilities among the four decision-making groups in every phase of the institution's operation.

[32] U.S. National Student Association, *1967–1968 Codification of Policy* (Washington, D.C., 1967) , pp., 51, 52, 54, 55.

Few institutions have yet implemented these demands, nor are they likely to do so. The student position ignores the lack of equal responsibility, even though the phrase is used lavishly; what they really want is mutual authority. Many presidents would probably like to share their responsibility, and may indeed delegate part of it to various individual students or groups on campus, but this does not diminish their accountability. It is unlikely that mutual authority will ever be successful; to the contrary, what is more likely to happen is a strong reaction against student demands. A taste of such a reaction was seen after the violence at Kent State over the Cambodia operation. Administrators now are adopting firm positions in the face of student demands on campus issues; at the same time they are acknowledging merit when it is evident. College presidents are remembering their accountability to trustees as well as to society.

No one can question that students arrive in college today with a greater awareness of social problems than was evident in previous generations. Nor can it be denied that in the past students worked under regulations that were more than slightly autocratic. This burning desire of today's students for mutual authority can be traced in part to an academic environment which was slow to change while the rest of the world was exposing young people to knowledge, good and bad, at an unheard-of rate. Knowledge has a way of demanding self-determination. But the newfound knowledge does not equip young people to set policy or to administer complex academic organizations. All their knowledge is from a world where total knowledge has expanded, leaving them still in the position of novices lacking in experience, talent, and time.[33]

This is not to say that presidents, and faculties as well, cannot benefit from the opinions of students in establishing policy. The students do have a contribution to make, and it is a real challenge to administrators and faculty members to develop this resource and to put it to good use. Morris Keeton has suggested a general principle for student (and faculty) involvement in institutional governance: "Design the role to obtain the contributions available from student competences and cooperation and to protect the other constituencies and the institutions against undue effects of the special interests and limitations that apply on the particular campus."[34]

It is important that administrators understand the distinction between student government attitudes and those of the student body

[33] Lewis B. Mayhew, *Arrogance on Campus* (San Francisco, Jossey-Bass, 1970), pp. 47–49.

[34] Keeton, *Shared Authority on Campus* (Washington, D.C.: American Association for Higher Education, 1971), p. 19.

generally. Student government typically advocates more extensive involvement in decisions than the student body expects. This is partly at the urging of national organizations such as USNSA and partly because student government officers are interested in campus affairs and consequently tend to promote the importance of their office. The average student probably will not desire much involvement as long as he feels his opinions are heard and respected or unless a crisis situation arises. Long-range planning is never effective under crisis conditions and is, in fact, partly intended as a means of avoiding expediency and emergency.

The students' demand for immediacy, if it is to have value, must be heard, filtered, channeled into the planning process, responded to, but not necessarily adhered to. The students' perspective of his institution is narrowed by his youth and brief exposure to the school. His demands should be received in this light, but they should not be ignored. A more responsive governance in higher education, as well as more attentive parents, public school teachers, ministers, and government officials, could have helped avoid the trauma of recent years. Seeking student opinion on policies is a matter of sound administration rather than of student rights, particularly in private schools, and hindsight, if nothing else, should tell us to be alert to student attitudes.

An architect wants his clients to accept his drawings and gets their opinions as he sketches, the doctor informs his patients of his prognoses to gain their cooperation, a business surveys consumers on product acceptance. Can a private college do any less? Administrators can be taught by students, and by their involvement can gain a cooperative environment in which learning, the "product," is improved.

The model proposed in this study is an administrative instrument to guide the decision makers in planning the future of the institution. Student input should be filtered through those who have accountability for their plans, but within this limitation students can be involved in establishing objectives, allocating resources, and evaluating effectiveness of components of the institution. The usefulness of the model is not deterred by the student movement; indeed it offers a logical means of responding to student needs.

3. Conclusions about Organization and Decision Making in Higher Education

In spite of the possibility of conflict in the dual system for educational policy, there was on all campuses a general understanding of what was expected from the faculty and the administration. There was some evidence, however, that a communications break often occurred when the financial feasibility question was raised with respect to curriculum changes.

Interviews with four different presidents indicated that their style of leadership had much to do with the relationship with both the faculty and the trustees. This was clearest in one president's comment that he believed in strong executive leadership. Another's concern about his nonacademic background called for a different type of leadership. The style of leadership seemed to be as crucial to faculty / administration relations as the substance of the program changes recommended by the four presidents.

Writers representing faculty, administration, and trustees indicate that such matters as approval of finances, property management, and public relations are the responsibility of the trustees but that the initiation of action and the recommendation and implementation of policy are generally delegated to the president. Individual faculty members have the freedom and with it the responsibility to conduct their classes, their research, their writing, and their speaking engagements as they choose. Between these two poles, however, there exists a range of matters generally referred to as educational policy which is claimed by each side, but with full awareness of the presence of the other. It is reasonable to suspect that in times of ample funding the faculty voice concerning educational policy goes relatively unchallenged but that in times of financial stringency there is a challenge with a loud but futile response by the faculty.

Although financial matters of an institution are within the control of the president and ultimately trustees, it is true that the fixed nature of the operating budget minimizes their influence in financial aspects of the educational program.

The factors governing jurisdiction over educational policy seem to be mostly subjective, such as the prestige of either the faculty, the administration, or the trustees, the relative forcefulness of each, the customs or precedence within each institution, the administrative competence of the president, or the prevailing attitudes of the academic world. The college president plays an important role in shaping this relationship, and in fact, the success of his administration may well depend on his awareness of the power structure that exists within his organization and how well he is able to shape it to the constructive ends of carrying out strategies.

It is also apparent that strategies to realize institutional missions result from stimulus by the president. The faculty serves the important role of sharpening the focus and providing new insights but seldom originates strategy. For this reason, the president has the greatest need for the proposed model, since his office is the origin of the action plans that result in strategic (long term) expenditures. He works with the faculty in carving out realistic educational strategies and with the trustees in identifying and allocating resources to these strategies. As the hub of the wheel he must stimulate the entire organization.

The field research conducted at the five participating schools substantiated the conclusions of the writers about the diffused nature of the decision-making process. Although no definitive recommendations can be offered to eliminate this situation, and perhaps none should be, there does seem to be reason for continued study of the organizational complexity in colleges and universities. The uncertainties created by this diffusion make the job of administering a college more difficult, and they make it even more important that attention be given to the problem of relating academic purposes to financial feasibility. "The framing and execution of long-range plans, one of the most important aspects of institutional responsibility, should be a central and a continuing concern in the academic community.[35] The financial planning model proposed here is intended to strengthen the overall planning process by providing an instrument through which the strategies for accomplishing the faculty's academic objectives can be related to financial feasibility as appraised by the trustees.

[35] "Statement on Government of Colleges and Universities," UVA A&P-1, p. 3.

EXHIBIT II.1. Miniversity A organization chart

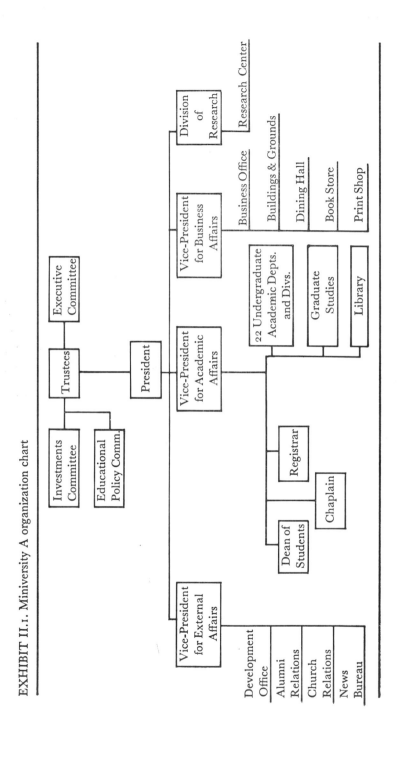

EXHIBIT II.2. Small college organization chart

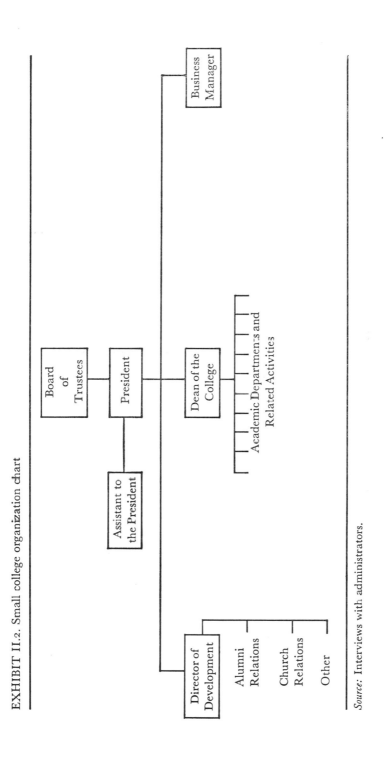

Source: Interviews with administrators.

EXHIBIT II.3. Miniversity B organization chart

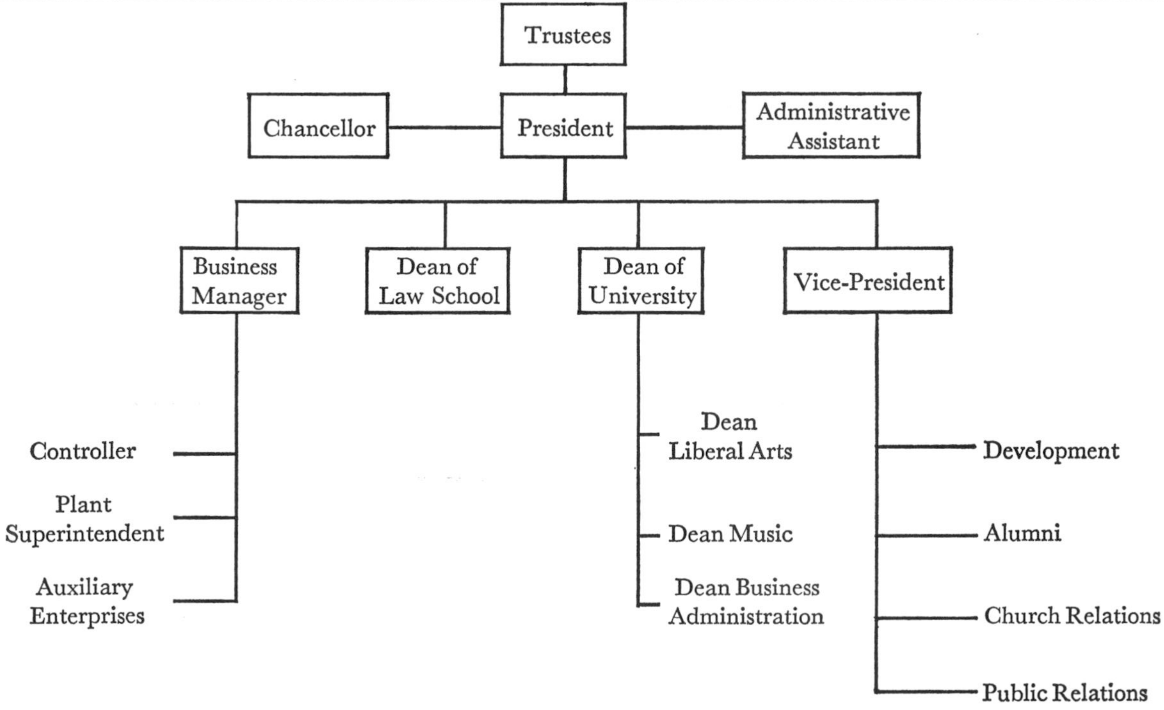

EXHIBIT II.4. Well-endowed college organization chart

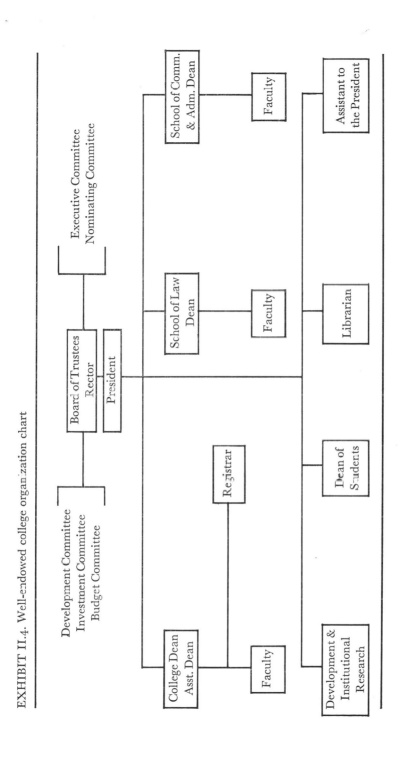

EXHIBIT II.5. Large university organization chart

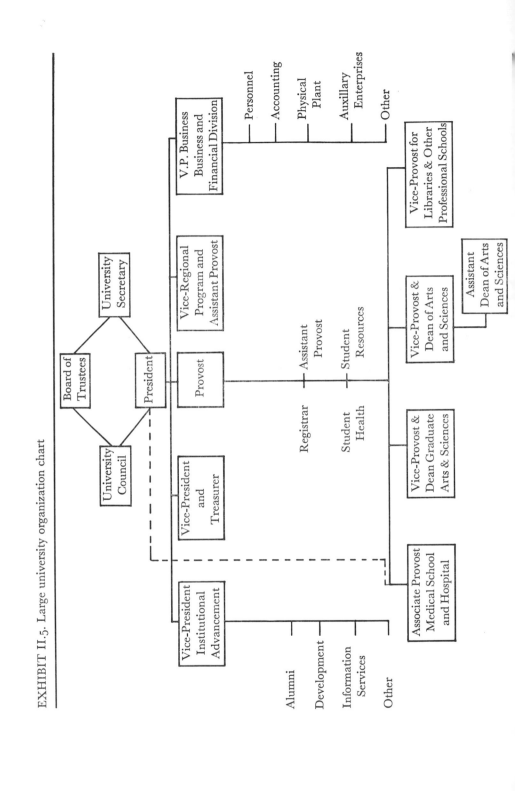

CHAPTER III

The Concepts of Strategy and Strategic Expenditures

T HE financial planning model presented here has three stages:

1. the identification of institutional strategies,
2. the classification of expenditures by strategies, and,
3. the computation of the quantitative measurement for evaluating the plans (later to be referred to as the utilization ratio) .

The techniques used and some of the terminology may be new to college administrators. The logic of the model focuses on financial elements in a different arrangement from the customary accounting or budgeting system found in higher education, or in most businesses for that matter. In this chapter the basic reasoning is explained, and the concepts of strategy and strategic expenditures are defined.

The operating budget of the typical private college or university contains a high proportion of expenditures that have been set by past decisions. For example, previous hiring, promotion, and retention decisions have determined the salaries of most of the faculty. Operating and maintenance costs incurred in running the physical plant are inescapable under normal conditions. In business terms, one would say there is a high proportion of fixed costs; that is, costs that do not vary with small changes in the level of operations or, in the case of colleges and universities, changes in the number of students. The college administrators who were interviewed estimated that these expenditures made up from 80 to 90 percent of the annual operating budget. Such fixed costs are not entirely uncontrollable, but it seems that colleges have fewer options available for reducing them than would normally be the case in industry.[1]

If the manager of a business decides to drop a product line, costs directly associated with the production and sale of the product can also be eliminated. Such direct control over costs is not possible in higher education. An uneconomical course may be dropped, but the

[1] Corson, in *Challenge and Change in American Education,* ed. Harris, Deitch, and Levensohn, pp. 236–37.

teacher's salary is not so easily eliminated, because of tenure interpretations. A normal salary expense in industry becomes a long-term commitment in colleges and universities. Because of their fixed nature, most expenditure commitments in higher education correspond to industry's long-term commitment to capital expenditures rather than to normal operating expenses. For this reason, industry's distinction between normal operating costs and long-term capital expenditures does not apply advantageously in higher education.

Industry generally has come to recognize that long-term capital expenditures are not controllable through operating budgets and has developed more appropriate control techniques through capital budgets. It is clear that colleges and universities must also get away from the annual operating budget as a control device over costs that are committed for several years into the future.

Long-range expenditures in business are evaluated in terms of their contribution to objectives, primarily to the ROI objective. The model proposed in this study is intended to fill a similar need in higher education, the need to evaluate the long-range plans for programs and projects in relation to financial objectives.

If this evaluation is to take place, abstract educational objectives must be transformed into specific programs and projects. An oversimplified statement of the financial objective in private higher education was suggested in the previous chapter: to offer a particular selection of courses and programs within the financial ability of the institution. Beyond this broad objective, it is still necessary to articulate institutional strategies, the first stage of the financial planning model.

Formulation of Institutional Strategy

Frequently private colleges make statements about their purpose in terms such as "to be a liberal arts college." Such statements cannot be converted into workable strategies to evaluate financial objectives. Businesses also have broad purposes, which Seymour Tilles has called the firm's mission, or "the fundamental purposes that the organization is trying to achieve."[2] All organizations have fundamental missions even though they are not always able to articulate them. It is not so apparent that organizations in business or higher education or elsewhere have reduced objectives to viable strategies.

[2] Tilles, "Strategies for Allocating Funds," *Harvard Business Review*, Jan.–Feb. 1966, p. 75.

The identification of these strategies is a necessary part of this research and a requirement of the proposed model.

The need to identify the general purpose of higher education and to classify purposes by functional missions was intensified by the development in this country of the university, where teaching is only one of several objectives. James A. Perkins, former president of Cornell University, identified three missions of the university and in doing so, provided the first tier in a hierarchy of objectives that can be useful in formulating strategies. First, he referred to the acquisition of knowledge as the mission of research; second, the transmission of knowledge as the mission of teaching; and, third, the application of knowledge as the mission of public service.[3]

The universities' and colleges' roles in teaching and basic research have historical foundations that need no amplification, but their role in public service programs has only recently been emphasized. Corson has suggested five reasons for their involvement:

1. Universities and colleges have the staff, facilities, endowment, climate, and prestige.
2. They have people with the particular talents and interests for solving social problems.
3. They have objectivity that participants in social action do not have.
4. They have a commitment to search for the truth.
5. They have ideals and they stand for values that will lend weight to their efforts.[4]

Although some of these reasons seem redundant (for instance, nos. 3 and 4), the substance of Corson's statement indicates that colleges and universities have a legitimate role in public service. It has been pointed out that each school should find its own niche in this area and be certain that its efforts accord with the institution's strategies in other areas. Each school should adopt strategies for public service for which it has the resources to fulfill a need.[5]

The concept of institutional strategy is drawn from the study of business policy and the process of formulating corporate strategy.[6]

[3] Perkins, *The University in Transition* (Princeton, N.J.: Princeton University Press, 1966), pp. 9–10.

[4] John J. Corson, "Public Service and Higher Education: Compatibility or Conflict," in *Whose Goals for American Higher Education,* ed. Charles G. Dobbins and Calvin B. T. Lee (Washington, D.C.: American Council on Education, 1968), pp. 83–87.

[5] Commentary on the Corson article by Roger Lebecha, "No University Should Become 'A Happening'," *ibid.,* p. 98.

[6] Edmund P. Learned, *et al., Business Policy, Text and Cases* (Homewood, Ill.: Richard D. Irwin, 1965), chap. 1.

It is an evolving concept even in industry and is an adaptation of the idea of military strategy. The formulation of strategy involves more than the setting of objectives; it also requires recognition of many constraints that tend to provide more realistic goals. These constraints can be seen in the following framework for formulating and implementing strategy adapted from the business policy literature.

1. Define feasible objectives
2. Analyze the elements of the environment in which the institution operates
3. Appraise and allocate resources, including money, people, facilities, and administrative and professional competence
4. Evaluate the personal values and style of the top administrators and faculty with due reference to the founder's purposes for the institution
5. Assess the risks and opportunities peculiar to the institution
6. Devise a structure that compliments the strategy: i.e., organizational relationships, information systems, position descriptions, performance measurement techniques, methods of selecting and training professional and administrative personnel, and a system of rewards compatible with the personnel employed

These factors can either restrict the institution as it pursues its broad objectives or be molded into a pattern that will allow the school to achieve greater success. Not every factor in the framework will be of equal importance in the consideration of an institution, and a full treatment of each one is outside the scope of this study. For this reason the framework is pertinent only when strategy formulation is expected to result in financial commitments. This will eliminate many objectives of substantial academic importance that do not, however, have major financial implications. In light of this parameter, the factors of the framework of prime interest to this study are the appraisal and allocation of resources (3), particularly financial resources, and the structural relationships (6) necessary to implement the proposed financial planning model.

The value of this framework comes from an understanding of the reason why it is evolving in business.[7] In the early years of corporate existence, businesses were usually single-purpose operations. There was perhaps one product manufactured in one plant with a relatively simple sales effort. There was a minimum of outside influence

[7] Alfred D. Chandler, Jr., *Strategy and Structure* (Cambridge, Mass.: M.I.T. Press, 1962); Alfred P. Sloan, Jr., *My Years with General Motors* (Garden City, N.Y.: Doubleday, 1964).

from government, unions, and social reform groups. Under these conditions, profit became the prime motivator and means of evaluation. As corporations became larger and more complex, it became less simple to relate all the necessary departments or divisions to profit contribution. Companies such as General Motors and Du Pont became multipurposed, with numerous divisions and plants, each with its own objectives, not all of which could be measured by ROI. This diversification created a need for a more unified means of giving direction to the organization; objectives were established in terms of something more than ROI.

In recent years great emphasis has been placed on the concept of "management by objective" in industry, and rightly so. Business is generally credited with being more objective-oriented than other organizations because of its history of profit motivation. In contrast to the early profit motivation, large diverse corporations are now finding ROI objectives inadequate for providing the proper direction to their business. They have developed lists of other objectives that sharpen the focus on purposes other than the profit requirement. For example, one large international company listed its objectives as:

to revitalize the sewing machine business,
to diversify the product line and reduce the over-all dependence on sewing machines, and
to affect a world-wide reorganization of the operating units of the company and their relations with one another and with the home office.[8]

Defining and implementing these objectives, establishing a structure to facilitate their accomplishment, and allocating resources while considering environmental opportunity and risk became the strategy adopted by this company.

Alfred D. Chandler, Jr., has defined strategy as "the determination of basic long-term goals and objectives of an enterprise, and the adoption of courses of action and the allocation of resources necessary for carrying out these goals." He further defined strategy simply as "the plan for the allocation of resources to anticipated demand."[9] One might call this concept an action plan. For a college or university, the strategies would be to allocate resources to the objective of accommodating society's demand for educational opportunities. For a private institution, this concept of strategies

[8] "The International Manufacturing Company" (B), ICH 9G250R, Harvard Business School, 1964, p. 1.
[9] Chandler, pp. 13, 383.

emphasizes the need to understand the constraints placed upon its objectives by limited resources.

It should be noted at this point that the plural word *strategies* is intended to refer to those specific programs and projects undertaken by a business or a college in the furtherance of its fundamental mission. They will be more detailed than those identified in the sewing machine company case but in total will reflect the same direction. The more detailed concept was found to be more useful for this research in relating expenditures to strategies.

A recent catalogue of one of the colleges contained this statement of mission:

Brunther College is committed to the Christian-democratic principle that every individual is of infinite worth within the brotherhood of mankind. On the basis of this principle its paramount objective is to enable the student to achieve the highest possible degree of self-realization and to make his greatest contribution to human welfare.

Brunther College endeavors to provide a program of liberal education, including a sound core of general studies consistent with the needs of youth in contemporary society, and such vocational courses as are in keeping with its resources and objectives.

To illustrate the concept of strategies, this broad mission may be compared to the following list of strategies implicit and explicit in the conduct of the administration.

1. To become a regional and residential school, as contrasted with its more local constituency of past years, attracting students from different social, economic, racial, ethnic, and religious environments

2. To accept undergraduate students whose high school performance ranks them in the middle third of their graduating class or above, if they can demonstrate other qualities that indicate potential success in college (This strategy does not diminish the efforts to attract top students as well.)

3. To require a well-rounded core of liberal arts courses of all students regardless of their major field emphases

4. To maintain the moral, ethical, and social standards of a church-related institution

5. To improve the weaker academic departments selectively through significant allocations of resources and to emphasize the academic strengths of the college

6. To improve the general academic program through the addition of high-caliber faculty and the establishment of funded faculty improvement programs

7. To encourage research by members of the faculty and staff who have the interest but at the same time to maintain emphasis on the primary college function of good teaching

8. To offer graduate work at the master's level in the fields where the college has competence and resources

9. To meet the community need for continuing education programs in addition to graduate education when it is compatible with community growth and the college's resources

10. To maintain the size of the undergraduate program between 1,500 and 2,000 students and to allow the graduate division to achieve its greatest foreseeable size

11. To seek actively funds to provide the facilities and other resources required by 1,500–2,000 students (This is manifest in the ten-year development program.)

12. To reorganize the college into three functional areas and within the academic affairs function to constitute twenty-two departments

13. To maintain the existing academic areas of study where there is a demand by a significant number of students, recognizing society's changing attitudes about education

Implications for Strategic Planning

The concepts of planning and allocation of resources appear throughout the discussion of strategy in business policy literature. For instance, this description of the Pentagon's procedures appeared in the *Harvard Business Review:*

Top management's primary job in any enterprise is the allocation of limited resources for selected mission purposes, in proper dimensions of time, for the furtherance of specified objectives.

D.O.D. [Department of Defense] . . . has worked to develop:

—Strategic planning by missions, allocating limited resources to each one, with plans assembled in a complete, carefully costed program package.

—A scheduled annual planning cycle, integrating strategy formulation with the budgeting process.[10]

Chandler made a distinction between strategic planning and day-to-day operating planning.

The formulation of policies and procedures can be defined as either strategic or tactical. *Strategic* decisions are concerned with the long-term

[10] Donald J. Smalter and Rudy L. Ruggles, "Six Business Lessons from the Pentagon," *Harvard Business Review*, March–April 1966, pp. 64–65.

health of the enterprise. *Tactical* decisions deal more with the day-to-day activities necessary for efficient and smooth operations. But decisions, either tactical or strategic, usually require *implementation* by an allocation or reallocation of resources—funds, equipment, or personnel. Strategic plans can be formulated from below, but normally the implementation of such proposals requires the resources which only the general office can provide. Within the broad policy lines laid down by that office and with the resources it allocates, the executives at the lower levels carry out tactical decisions.[11]

Strategic plans may be formulated from below as Chandler said, but it is doubtful that this sort of planning occurs more than two or three levels into the lower management echelons, and then only in the largest companies. Lower-level management does not have the authority over resources to implement strategy (Chandler's point), but in addition their responsibility is usually clearly enclosed within the parameters of job descriptions, job titles, or limited delegation of authority from superiors. Therefore, in practice there is little difference between Chandler's concept of strategic planning and Tilles's statement that: "what is increasingly needed is a way of thinking about fund allocation that permits the company to be considered as a whole and from the top down, rather than as a collection of pieces from the bottom up."[12]

Another author described the difficulty that companies have in thinking in terms of strategic planning: "plans only describe what happens if the company continues the business policies already in effect. No one is working on the policies themselves. The controller's plans are operating plans and not strategic plans."[13] What is needed is a broad systems approach to strategic planning by top management with the authority to implement programs involving the long-term health of the enterprise.

If this need can be observed in industry, it should be even more obvious in private colleges and universities, which are committed to greater proportions of fixed costs. A system is required that identifies realistic strategies as well as plans for the allocation of resources. This type of strategic planning is suggested in a Research Report sponsored by the Danforth Foundation.

Church [educational] institutions sorely need models of their own to serve as broad conceptual frameworks. These should provide internally consistent patterns of purpose and program, not as blueprints to be followed

11 P. 11.

12 *Harvard Business Review*, Jan.–Feb. 1966, p. 75.

13 Robert Mainer, "The Case of the Stymied Strategist," *Harvard Business Review*, May–June 1968, p. 40.

slavishly by institutions—we have already inveighed against imitation—but as illustrations of the proper relationship of ends and means.[14]

It seems reasonable that this statement can apply to all private institutions, whether they are church-related or independent.

With the decision-making responsibility diffused among faculty, administration, and trustees, it is important that institutional strategies be formulated and clearly identified for all three groups. Without such guidance individuals in the organization, not knowing exactly what is expected of them, will work toward objectives of their own. This is particularly true in organizations composed primarily of professionals.[15] The importance of strategic planning to private higher education is also accentuated by the limited resources available. This limitation makes it imperative that the maximum contribution to strategies is obtained from these scarce financial resources.

The allocation of resources to strategies is referred to here as strategic expenditures. When implementation of a particular strategy results in expenditures for assets, additional people, or other items that would not otherwise have been made, these can be identified as strategic expenditures. This term was only found in use in one other source, a large company in which "strategic expenditures"

(sometimes called "policy expenditures") include those expenses which are necessary to make provisions for achieving the long-range objectives of the business. . . . Examples would include projects with the following purposes:
1. To develop new products,
2. To exploit new markets,
3. To improve existing products,
4. To reduce cost and operating expense,
5. To increase capital turnover,
6. To reduce lead times,
7. To improve marketing methods and distribution,
8. To advertise the company and its products,
9. To increase capacity or utilize existing capacity.

Although strategic expenditures cover a wide variety of projects, there is one basic objective in mind: To enhance the future strength of the company and its ability to compete profitably.[16]

---

[14] Manning M. Pattillo, Jr., and Donald M. Mackenzie, *Church-sponsored Higher Education in the United States,* Report of the Danforth Commission (Washington, D.C.: American Council on Education, 1966), p. 215.

[15] Corson, in Harris, Deitch, and Levensohn, eds., pp. 236–37.

[16] William Rotch, "United Electronics Corporation" (A), UVa-C-355, Sponsors of the Graduate School of Business Administration, University of Virginia, 1966, pp. 2–3.

The Department of Defense (DOD) in the early 1960s made a major contribution toward the concept of segmenting the total mission into programs. Strategic expenditures are quite similar to DOD's programs in that each may cut across a number of decision points (academic departments or schools, administrative decision centers, and so on). Within DOD, for instance, the budgets of the army, navy, air force, and NASA each have a major section for the space program, and presumably each branch distributes its entire budget to the programs requested. If for some reason Congress decided to discontinue the space program, that portion of the budget of each branch would be cut. If a new program was added by DOD, the funds for it would be added to the budget of those branches which would implement it.

In an effort to apply the DOD experience to higher education, Harry Williams has suggested that colleges establish schools and other "collection (s) of integrated resources" as programs. He proposes further that program elements could then be established as "a combination of related resources which enables a student to pursue a particular objective; it might more commonly be defined as a particular department . . . within a school or college."[17] It would also seem that a major within a department or school could be considered a program element.

Williams missed a fundamental point, however, in his attempt to apply the DOD concept to higher education. For the government, the space program can be viewed as incremental at the will of Congress. This is not necessarily true of a school, a department, or a major in higher education, however. The program itself may be discontinued, but the costs associated with it, such as salaries of tenured faculty, will not automatically disappear. The basic difference between the DOD (and Williams's) program and the concept of strategic expenditures proposed in this study results from the difference between incremental and on-going expenditures. The proposed program includes both strategic expenditures that are incremental in the sense that a change in plans before commitment can change the expenditure level and strategic expenditures for ongoing program elements, which will not necessarily change when plans are altered.

The model focuses attention on strategies that require positive action by administrators within the planning period and on the incremental allocation of resources to these strategies (incremental

[17] Williams, *Planning for Effective Resource Allocation in Universities* (Washington, D.C.: American Council on Education, 1966), p. 7.

strategic expenditures). The final category of expenditures will be for the on-going strategy of continuing the existing programs. These expenditures will be for programs previously committed and will allow fewer options to administrators for controlling them. Occasionally an institution will have an opportunity to terminate an on-going strategic expenditure, for instance, through normal attrition of faculty. This is also a long-range planning problem and can be adopted as a strategy using the model proposed in this research.

The allocation of resources will be expressed in financial terms, but it should be remembered that in any organization, particularly a college or university, there are intangible resources that cannot be expressed financially. These very important resources are outside the parameter of this study, which is only concerned with financial planning.

The Financial Planning Model

Exhibit III.1 presents the three-dimensional financial planning model. Financial resources are first allocated to strategies, which are identified by column headings. The total for each column then becomes the strategic expenditures necessary to accomplish the particular strategy. The financial resources to be allocated, the revenue by sources, is also represented by columns on the right-hand side of the matrix. In the long run, the sum of the strategic expenditure columns is expected to equal the sum of the strategic revenue columns.

The rows across the matrix contain summary amounts representing the amount of the strategic expenditures that will be committed by the various responsibility centers within the institution. These centers may be academic departments, separate schools, administrative departments, or capital expenditure projects. Since the on-going strategy of continuing existing programs is included, the total of the strategic expenditures for a given row can be used as a control of the planned departmental budgets and of the capital expenditure budgets. The significance of this point is worth reiterating: the long-range strategic expenditures from the model are intended to be a control over the annual operating and capital budgets in order to assure that all expenditures are contributing to the total mission as segmented into workable strategies.

Many strategies adopted by a college or university may be aimed at generating revenue necessary to offer a program or to undertake a project. Special efforts may be made to obtain larger amounts of federal funds as well as grants from private foundations. Further, certain programs for which strategic expenditures may be required will also generate income, e.g., a new graduate program or a center for noncredit offerings. These revenue-producing strategies must be incorporated into the revenue constraints on the right-hand side of the matrix.

The third dimension in the matrix, the depth axis, represents the number of years in the planning period. Assuming that asset replacement and expansion are included in the projects planned by the institution, revenue minus strategic expenditures (including the expenditures for continuing existing programs) is expected, in the long run, to equal zero. Economic price level changes and growth in existing programs make it necessary to build increases in future years' strategic expenditures and revenue into the model.

In business "the two-fold objective of financial management is to maximize net present value or wealth by seeing that cash is on hand to pay bills on time, and to assist in the most profitable allocation of resources within the firm."[18] These objectives concern both profitability and solvency. Private colleges and universities, on the other hand, are only concerned with solvency, which implies the need for a cash-flow analysis. To measure solvency, borrowed funds are treated in the model as receipts in the year received, and repayments are included in a strategic expenditure in each of the years of repayment.

The result of this cash-flow approach is that strategic expenditures minus cash inflow will equal zero in each year, rather than having the zero balance occur at the end of the planning period as shown in Exhibit III.1.[19] The zero balance is probably realistic only in the long run, but for planning purposes it is vital to know the amount that will have to be borrowed or the amount of surplus each year. The year-by-year zero balance forces administrators to ascertain sources of loan repayment that will affect later years' cash flow.

Given the zero constraint and the rates of growth and price level changes, strategic financial planning becomes a matter of asking: If we adopt a particular strategy and this strategy requires the expenditure of resources (not all strategies will), what will be the source of these resources? Can we increase the number of students to be enrolled, increase the tuition rate, obtain a grant, borrow the funds, or reduce the proposed commitment to some other strategy? The problem becomes one of deciding the most beneficial trade-off

[18] Johnson, p. 10.

[19] This assumes a level cash balance during each year and throughout the planning period. An excess cash balance could also be included in the model as a source of funds, and a deficit balance could be a use of funds.

within the three constraining dimensions of time, strategic expenditures, and sources of funds.

The quantitative measure proposed as part of the three-stage model is intended to measure the financial effects of various sets of strategies. As administrators attempt to balance the academic mission against financial constraints, the quantitative measure will require them to trade-off the programs for which there is public demand against those that are financially feasible.

Other types of long-range planning or budgeting have been proposed for higher education, but they are fragmented, encumbered with massive detail, and do not clearly reflect the relationship of expenditures to objectives.[20]

James B. Conant, former president of Harvard, recognized three requisites for the successful operation of a university: solvency, a student body of high quality, and an outstanding faculty.[21] The first requisite, solvency, requires financial planning that facilitates the formulation of strategies aimed at obtaining the student body and faculty. Often private college administrators do not have the background, organizational support, or the resources to cope with the solvency problem. The financial planning model proposed here is intended to help overcome this problem by providing a framework for formulating, implementing, and evaluating institutional strategies for the allocation of financial resources.

[20] Sidney G. Tickton, *Needed: A Ten-Year College Budget* (New York: The Fund for the Advancement of Education, 1961).

[21] *The University and Its Resources* (Cambridge, Mass.: Harvard University Press, 1968.

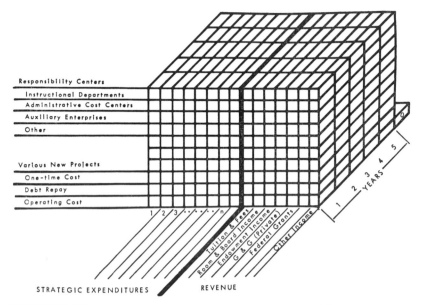

EXHIBIT III.1. Graphic design of financial planning model

CHAPTER IV

The Model Described

THE model conceptualized in Chapter III still remains to be applied. In the original research, the model was first applied in one private miniversity and then tested at four other schools with different characteristics. The three stages of the model can best be demonstrated by describing the process of application at the original institution, miniversity A, to be referred to as Brunther College. Some of the history of the college and its characteristics (Exhibit IV.1) may aid in explaining the logic of various elements in the model.

Since its founding near the turn of the twentieth century, the college has had five major presidents—all of which were selected from its Protestant denominational constituency. Like many denominational colleges, its existence has been marked by a number of major crises, and its evolution seems to have progressed from strength gained through these experiences.

In the early years, financial problems beset the founder and first president. The initial efforts to achieve denominational acceptance met with little success, and income depended on student tuition. This condition existed in various degrees for the first fifty years. Numerous campaigns were necessary to reduce indebtedness and to meet operating expenses.

The nature of the church relationship was debated by faculty and trustees alike, reaching a climax in the 1920s when the advocates of a "Bible College" concept were defeated narrowly by the proponents of the liberal arts. Although the issue did not end there, the abstract standards of a liberal arts education have since then been used to determine the direction of the academic program.

The college was accredited in 1927 by the regional accrediting agency. There was one interruption of the accreditation in the early 1940s because of what was considered an excessive debt of $240,000. When the college was admitted to the regional association, it was given membership upon the condition that it would reduce its indebtedness. When the examining committee of the accrediting association made its investigation of the college in the mid-1930s, it complimented the academic program but looked with concern upon the debt. The college was unable to reduce its indebtedness, and it was placed on probation by the association on April 30, 1938. This probation was made even more definite in December 1941, when the executive secretary of the association wrote the president of Brunther College:

the recommendation of the Committee on Reports was as follows:

"The Committee voted to continue the institution on probation for failure to meet the standards of the association."

"A minimum reduction of indebtedness to the amount of $50,000 will have to be made by December, 1942."

The challenge of the debt was clear, and in due course the crisis was averted by another money-raising campaign.

The dean of Brunther College, who has served as an examiner for the association on numerous occasions, indicated that schools have frequently been placed on probation for excessive debt, although the association seldom publicizes the reason for probation. He stated that frequently the examining committee would apply probationary strictures for the good of the school and to awaken trustees to the dangers of excessive debt. The standards for accreditation set by the regional association make no specific mention to debt levels but do include such general statements as: "Planning should include specific projections of income from each source, specific plans for major categories of expenditure, and plans for the increase of capital resources."[1]

This relationship of excessive debt to accreditation creates an even greater need for study of debt capacity at private colleges and universities.

At the same time as the accreditation interruption, the college embarked on its initial vocational education efforts in business administration. From this point on, the educational objectives have been in two directions—vocational and liberal arts. Considerable energy and thought have been directed toward the college's proper position in these two efforts.

During the Korean conflict, another financial crisis developed when the war effort limited student enrollment. It was at this point that the college received its first large gift from an estate, which not only resolved the immediate problem but seemed to inject new life and spirit into the campus.

The college had reached a strategic position by the mid-1960s;

[1] *Standards of the College Delegate Assembly* of the Southern Association of Colleges and Schools, 795 Peachtree Road, N.E., Atlanta, Ga. 30308, Nov. 29, 1967.

for the first time it had the resources, in addition to the leadership, to assume a greater voice in its own destiny. No longer was every decision a reaction to some crisis or expediency; instead there was time to take a longer-range view of the direction of the school and plan its future.

Brunther College was private; it was not directly controlled by the federal, state, or local governments. There was federal support which amounted to about 3 percent of the total operating income during the year ended June 30, 1968; this support was expected to be an increasing source of income. The academic emphasis was and is expected to remain on undergraduate education. The graduate program was limited to programs aimed at meeting specific local demands, and research was restricted to the interests of particular faculty members, as opposed to major contracts made by the institution. Public service projects were undertaken in a small way by the college and by members of the faculty and staff. These characteristics seem to make Brunther College a miniversity.

There were about 1,500 undergraduate students by 1967–68, with approximately 250 part-time graduate students and 100 faculty members. As of June 30, 1967, total assets were recorded at $8.9 million, endowment at $2.3 million, and annual revenue for the previous school year was $2.3 million. More detailed financial data are presented in Exhibits IV.2 and IV.3.

The college's church relationship can best be described using the six elements set forth in Table I.2.

1. Board composition: As of October 1967, the college's charter was amended to remove the requirement that a majority of trustees be from the denomination. Only the by-laws continued to have this requirement.

2. Ownership: Brunther College had recently been incorporated as a private nonprofit educational institution and now holds the title to its assets, enters into contracts, and conducts its affairs in its own name with the trustees acting as the official agents. The denomination has no official voice in the governance of the college.

3. Financial support: About 2–3 percent of the current funds at the college are received from the denomination and individual churches. In addition, church members have made significant donations and special campaigns have provided capital funds. About 200 students from denomination families are enrolled each year.

4. Acceptance of the denominational standards: Traditionally the leadership of the college has been drawn from the denomi-

nation. This has tended to make the moral, social, and ethical standards of the college approach those of the denomination. However, specific denomination doctrine is neither taught nor required.

5. Connection with the denomination through a statement of purpose in the charter, by-laws, or other published documents: There is no stated purpose of educating only young people from the denomination nor is there a special effort to train young people for the specific ministry. The ministerial training program is closer to the denomination in practice than in purpose. The relationship is primarily for the purposes of financial support and the church-related image.

6. Selection of administrators and faculty from the denomination: There is no statutory requirement that faculty or staff be selected from the denomination; however, all past presidents have been from the denomination, as have been all of the academic deans, a significant number of the present faculty, and a substantial number of staff members.

Strategies at Brunther College (Stage 1 of the Model)

With this background we can now turn to the major purpose of this research, to offer a methodology in the form of the three-stage model for financial planning. The first stage, identifying institutional strategies, has been illustrated with a list of the thirteen objectives of Brunther College given in Chapter III and now repeated in Exhibit IV.4 for formal reference purposes. The analysis of Brunther's objectives here is intended to illustrate the application of the framework for strategy formulation; it is not the purpose to criticize the college's administration or their objectives. Five strategies will be discussed in detail to show how the analytical framework can be used. In a later section of this chapter, all thirteen objectives will be incorporated into the financial analysis.

Strategy 1

To become a regional and residential school, as contrasted with its more local constituency of past years, attracting students from different social, economic, racial, ethnic, and religious environments

It could be argued that this was a strategy of every school, but at Brunther College it represented a conscious switch in emphasis. Conversations with the president and dean revealed a number of reasons for this strategy. The major one was competition from the state-supported, two-year community college that had recently been established in the city.

In becoming a regional school, Brunther College would draw students from a wider area, making it necessary for a larger proportion of the student body to live in on-campus facilities, which had to be built. The college had never been totally a local institution since it had always drawn students from a regional church constituency, but the new strategy meant an increase in the percentage of out-of-state students (Table IV.1).

TABLE IV.1. Brunther College enrollment by states, 1958–59 and 1968–69

	1958–59		1968–69	
	Number[a]	%	Number[a]	%
Home state	624	83.5	1,220	65.9
Maryland	11	1.4	107	5.8
North Carolina	8	1.1	18	1.0
West Virginia	5	.7	5	.2
Florida	39	5.2	27	1.5
New Jersey	7	1.0	232	12.5
New York	5	.7	82	4.5
Pennsylvania	6	.8	49	2.6
Indiana	6	.8	1	—
Washington, D.C.	5	.7	7	.3
All other states and foreign countries	31	4.1	106	5.7
Total	747	100.0%	1,854	100.0%

Source: Records from the registrar's office, Brunther College.

[a] Includes evening and special students.

The administration also reasoned that a more regional image would have a greater appeal to the faculty; they felt that prospective faculty members were attracted by the opportunity to teach a diverse student body.

Closely related to this strategy is strategy 10.

Strategy 10

To maintain the size of the undergraduate program between 1,500 and 2,000 students and to allow the graduate division to achieve its greatest foreseeable size

This strategy was based upon a belief that there was an optimum size which would allow the college to afford the facilities, faculty, and funds to become a top-rate institution. Normally, the size of a student body can be increased—even doubled—without having to double the library resources, gymnasium, student activities building, and other services necessary at a residential school. Since Brunther College already had to improve or expand these service resources, the feeling was that they should also provide for an increased student body that would allow them to operate at an optimum level. At the time the strategy was adopted, the president felt that the college needed to make a major capital investment in buildings, such as a dining hall, a student center, an athletic facility, additional dormitories, and a library addition. There were about 700 students at the college, and with a small endowment, there was little chance of fulfilling such a major construction program. It was decided to look for federal funds in the form of grants and loans where possible, as well as private gifts, but also to plan for an expansion to about 1,500 to 2,000 students. With this large a student body, the college felt that it could afford the capital program and the debt service would not be such a large proportion of the annual budget.

When these two strategies are tested against other elements in the framework, the difficulties of implementing them can be observed. If the college's resources had been realistically appraised, the question could have been raised whether even 1,500–2,000 students could support the addition to the physical plant necessary to become a regional institution. The potential conflict between objectives and resources, in the form of pressure for higher tuition, will become more apparent as the quantitative stages of the model, the second and third steps, are developed.

Both strategies 1 and 10 indicate a need for dormitories. In light of this, several administrators at the college questioned the kind of housing the college should offer. The environment from which the increased student body would be selected was undergoing changing values. The parietal control expected of colleges in the past seemed to be disappearing. With these changes, the usual architectual style for student housing was becoming one that allowed them more independence. In addition, the efforts to attract a more diverse student body had to be evaluated in relation to their different environmental backgrounds. Could the college offer programs and living conditions that would be equally attractive to students from north and middle Atlantic states as well as from southern states?

Comparison of strategy 4 and strategy 10 raises another question of potential conflict.

Strategy 4

To maintain the moral, ethical, and social standards of a church-related institution

There was little doubt that this policy was a long-standing objective, but there were different emphases among faculty members at Brunther College, as there were among the many church-related institutions. This strategy did not mean imposing specific attitudes, denominational beliefs and doctrine, or religious obligations on either students or faculty. It did indicate the college's desire to enrich the campus religious life as part of its obligation as a liberal arts school. A recently constructed chapel and the newly hired chaplain were evidence of resource allocations to this strategy.

Within the constituency from which the college had previously attracted students, strategy 4 was accepted without question. But among students and faculty attracted from more diverse backgrounds, conformity could be expected to be more difficult to achieve in the future. In fact, there was some question of whether conformity should be required or even desired. Were the values of the founders and present leadership in conflict with those brought to the campus by students and faculty under strategy 1? Was the faculty sufficiently adaptable to cope with the more diverse student body? Across the country a shift away from traditional church involvement has been evident for some time, particularly on campuses like Brunther College. A great deal of the change in attitude resulted from recruiting from the more diverse regions of the East. An early awareness of this potential effect might have lessened its extent and made it possible to allocate the faculty and staff resources more effectively. At any rate, it is important to consider the mission of a private institution when offering employment to faculty members or admission to students.

Another potential inconsistency between objectives and resources can be observed by the comparison of strategy 8 and strategy 10.

Strategy 8

To offer graduate work at the master's level in the fields where the college has competence and resources

There was no disagreement on this strategy, initiated before this study was begun. The graduate programs were almost entirely evening or part-time offerings and were restricted to the fields of education, physics, and business administration, all of which answered community needs. Any expansion of the graduate programs was also expected to answer specific and identifiable needs and to come in a manner which would not detract from the undergraduate program.

Since members of the undergraduate faculty were to teach many of the graduate courses, they would either be required to teach overloads or to reduce their teaching load at the undergraduate level. There was a strong effort to keep overall teaching loads at a normal level (four courses per semester) ; consequently strategy 8 meant that the professors in graduate courses were not available for undergraduate work or at least were only available part time. There are financial implications of this situation, but perhaps more important, the graduate program tended to take many of better-qualified teachers out of the undergraduate program. If undergraduate education was to be the major emphasis, there was a potential conflict for the services of the terminal degree holders on the faculty between the undergraduate program and the graduate courses.

One additional strategy can be used to illustrate the application of the framework.

Strategy 11

To seek actively funds to provide the facilities and other resources required by 1,500–2,000 students

There could be little argument with the college's need for such funds, and in fact, a number of federal grants and loans had been obtained. The value in analyzing this strategy in terms of the elements in the framework outlined in Chapter III comes from considerations of the environment in which it is to be implemented. Wealthy alumni and friends of an institution are generally viewed as the source of endowment funds, but at Brunther College the alumni and friends were largely ministers, teachers, government employees, and middle managers in business. In addition, only in recent years had the college generated large numbers of graduates. These facts tend to make campaigns for financial support difficult.

In addition, support for endowment is seldom available from foundations or from the government. Of course, capital from these two sources is available, but it is limited to specific building projects or special educational, research, or public service programs. The college had obtained government funds for these purposes, and they were expected to continue. But government grants seldom provide all of the capital required, and they do not provide funds for the continued operation of buildings or programs after the initial grant. This means, for a private college such as Brunther, that additional funds must be procured from private donors, operating income, or debt, which has to be repaid from operating income. Application of the framework raises the question whether other strategies, such as 1 and 10, should be implemented before the funds of strategy 11 are at least reasonably expected. Normally it would seem more realistic to adopt strategies for sources of income simultaneously with strategies for the allocation of resources. The Brunther College administrators did not ignore the risk in their approach but accepted it in order to take advantage of the timely opportunities for federal funds.

The inconsistencies revealed by this analysis illustrate the use of the framework and the need for internal consistency in the institutional strategy. Objectives should not conflict with one another. The realities of available resources must be considered in relationship to environmental constraints, and structurally there should be compatability between the organization, its many units, and the objective. The Brunther College administration did consider many of the questions raised here; they carefully appraised the risks inherent in the strategies; and after considering the best available information, they decided to adopt the bold, dynamic plans.

The evaluation of the risks apparent in the dynamic long-range plans was based on traditional concepts of financing and budgeting in higher education. The long-range effects on the college's financial structure could only be evaluated subjectively, for the model proposed in this study was not available. Had it been used, the ultimate effect of the rising pressure on revenue derived from current sources, particularly student tuition, could have been determined from the quantitative measure presented in the next section.

Classification of Strategic Expenditures (Stage 2)

The three-stage model is intended to be used in long-range planning of strategic expenditures and in determining the ability to finance them out of cash revenue and/or debt. The second and third stages of the model, both quantitative, consist of classifying all expenditures for programs and capital projects according to the strategies identified in the first stage (in other words, determining strategic expenditures) and computing the ultimate measure—to be called the utilization ratio (UR).

In classifying strategic expenditures at Brunther College, the reason for each expenditure was determined from accounting records, capital expenditure proposals, other source documents, and conversations with college officials. With this information, expenditures were assigned to strategies as shown in Exhibit IV.5a. The columns represent the thirteen strategies identified at the college and the rows represent summary figures for on-going and incremental programs and projects. In this manner, all expected expenditures were assigned to a strategic expenditure and to a program or project.

In some cases it was necessary to allocate expenditures to more than one strategy. For instance, the cost of additional recruiters in the admissions office was assigned to strategy 10, expanding the size of the college to 1,500–2,000 students, and the remainder of the admissions office expense was assigned to strategy 13, maintaining existing programs.[2] All costs that could not be incrementally identified with a specific strategy were assigned to 13 under the assumption that these costs were the result of the existing program.

The total of columns 1 through 12 represents the strategic expenditures applicable to the college's incremental strategies. The on-going strategy, 13, was also clearly part of the long-range plans since there was no intention of significantly reducing programs that were in demand.

The expenditures assigned to strategies 1 through 12 are incremental in the sense that a decision to drop one of them, before commitment, would make it possible to reduce costs by the amount of that column. Once a strategy has been implemented and its success is reasonably assured, its incremental nature may cease. For instance, the initiation of an MBA program at Brunther was incremental at the time of the study. But as the program continued and the new faculty members were given tenure, the incremental nature was lost. Therefore, in future years when the schedule of strategic expenditures is prepared, the new MBA program should be transferred to the on-going strategic expenditure column. This process emphasizes the importance of deciding before commitment which strategies are incremental and financially feasible and which should be eliminated from the plan.[3]

In the lower part of Exhibit IV.5a, revenue was also identified with strategies when the income could be anticipated with a reasonable degree of certainty. The need for developing strategies on the source of income is already apparent. Some strategies created strategic income, e.g., strategy 8, to offer graduate work. In addition, strategies that included building projects frequently were expected to be partially financed by federal and private grants. When funds were

[2] This could be done since it was known that certain recruiters were employed only after strategy 10 was adopted and that they were assigned areas not typically covered by Brunther College.

[3] It was stated previously that administrators are not entirely without options to eliminate academic programs. If, for example, the MBA program proved undesirable in some future year, the business administration department would probably have too many teachers. Although they could not be terminated immediately, it would be possible through long-range planning to reduce the size of the department faculty by not replacing teachers who left, by not hiring new men, by retirement, or by other gradual means. This type of planning should be as much a part of the model as planning for constantly growing programs.

to be borrowed, the amount of the loan was also shown as part of the strategy—a form of strategic receipts.[4] The undesignated non-tuition revenue from all other sources was assigned to strategy 13 for much the same reason as were the expenditures for on-going programs.[5]

The net result of subtracting all nontuition income and borrowed funds from the total strategic expenditures gives the net difference to be paid by student tuition. It should be noted that strategic expenditures without identifiable sources of financing result in an increase in the required tuition revenue. For private colleges, such as Brunther College, that have limited nontuition sources of income and are competing with state-supported institutions for students, the change in the amount of student tuition needed is critical.

The time element was brought into the model by the number of years in the long-range planning period. In Exhibit IV.5a, the amounts represent the total strategic expenditures or revenue for a five-year period. These total figures become the control with which the annual figures in Exhibit IV.5b must accord. The annual data are necessary to show the trend in the ultimate UR and to account for changes in either the cash balance or the amount borrowed or repaid.

Any number of years could be selected without changing the methodology of the computation. A study sponsored by the Ford Foundation, through the Fund for the Advancement of Education, recommended a ten-year budget for higher education.[6] Some of the administrators interviewed felt that guesswork entered in beyond five years; for this reason the five-year period was used at Brunther and at two of the test schools. At another institution, the five-year period was not long enough to ascertain the full effect of its strategies, and an eight-year period was used.

Certainly, it is clear that effective control over long-range expenditures can hardly be exercised with one-year operating budgets. A longer period must be selected in order to provide perspective on the effect of long-range commitments on the financial strength of the institution. The period selected should be determined by the pur-

[4] Since borrowed funds were shown as receipts in the year received, it was also necessary to show repayment of principal and interest as part of future years' strategic expenditures. In this way, a decision to exclude a strategy (in the planning stage) may have an effect over several years.

[5] The number of students planned for the dormitories and dining hall was a percentage of capacity ranging from 97 percent at the beginning of each year to 90 percent at the end of the year.

[6] Tickton.

pose for long-range planning: it should be long enough to allow observation of the full effect of strategic planning on future solvency. For instance, the time period should not be cut off in five years if a new program is expected to reach maturity in seven years.

Computation of the Utilization Ratio (Stage 3)

The third, and final, step in the financial planning model is the computation of the utilization ratio (UR). In this step, shown in Table IV.2, the net difference to be paid by students is divided by

TABLE IV.2. Computation of utilization ratio proposed for 1968–73 at Brunther College

	Net differ- ence[a]	Average tuition rate	Students required	Student capacity	UR
	(in 1000's)				
1968–69	$2,057	$1,340	1,535	2,025	.758
1969–70	2,380	1,370	1,737	2,025	.857
1970–71	2,514	1,390	1,809	2,025	.893
1971–72	2,803	1,400	2,002	2,025	.988
1972–73	3,084	1,400	2,203	2,025	1.087

[a] Figures are taken from Exhibit IV.5b.

the average tuition rate to determine the number of students required to accomplish the plans called for in the college's list of strategies. The number of students required is then divided by the planned student capacity to determine the rate at which the college is utilizing its facilities—the UR. The model for calculating the UR can also be demonstrated mathematically using the variables listed in the Appendix.

Estimates of each year's tuition rate were the average expected to be paid by students enrolled in those years. Brunther College offered its students a four-year proposed tuition rate which the college tried to maintain, although it did not guarantee the rate. The college planned to continue this inducement. Such a rate structure meant that if tuition rates were changed annually, the student body might be paying four different rates.

The calculation of student capacity used in the UR is subject to different interpretations and needs amplification. There is no real fixed capacity in a college or university. Even in dormitories the number of students housed in each room can be varied, and off-campus housing can be secured. Beyond the residence capacity, the computation of institutional capacity is even more nebulous. Factors that enter into this computation might include the number of classrooms, their size, the class hours scheduled for them, the number of evening school courses, the number of days per week of instruction, summer programs, and faculty attitude toward class size.[7] For a given school, the only reasonable approach is to develop capacity under the conditions planned for the foreseeable future, giving, not a true capacity, but a planned capacity which the institution might vary if expected conditions changed significantly.

No previous attempt had been made to define planned capacity at Brunther College, but there were reasonably clear estimates of the capacity in the dormitories (based on two students to a room) and dining hall. For the purpose of this study, the smaller of classroom size or professors' attitude concerning class size was used as the capacity for each course offered during three semesters, fall and spring, 1967–68, and fall, 1968–69. The average of these three semesters produced a planned capacity of 2,025 (Exhibit IV.6). This figure is an average which assumes that the distribution of students among courses will be the same as it is at the time of the capacity calculation, an unlikely event. Therefore, the 2,025 average is valid only as a planning device, and in fact, a UR goal of something less than 100 percent—say 90 percent—may be more realistic.

The most recent three semesters were used at Brunther College because the enrollment, size of faculty, and classroom space seemed to have reached the desired levels during that period. The use of earlier semesters would have lowered the capacity figure unrealistically.

At Brunther College, there was great emphasis on small classes with a close relationship between faculty and students. Consequently, the faculty attitude concerning their class size was the constraining influence in determining planning capacity. At schools located away from urban areas from which off-campus students can commute, the planned capacity may be constrained by the dormitory and dining hall capacity.

The number of classroom seats is not likely to be a constraint. At Brunther College, there were approximately 1,300 classroom seats. If the evening hours are excluded (which is not totally realistic),

[7] At each participating college, it was found that one constraint usually determined capacity. At one college dormitory space was the limitation, but at another the constraint was the size of the faculty plus the philosophy that emphasized smaller classes.

there were eight class periods per day and five days of classes per week. The average course load for a student was about five per semester, in which he attended class two and one-half hours per week in each course.[8] Using these figures, the student capacity was

$$\frac{1,300 \times 8 \times 5 \text{ days}}{5 \text{ courses} \times 2\frac{1}{2} \text{ hrs.}} = 4,176.$$

But the college did not have a faculty large enough to support 4,176 students. In addition, many faculty members resisted teaching classes as large as the size their classroom would have allowed. For this reason, the size of the faculty and their attitude about class size were the major determining constraints on planned capacity at Brunther College. The word *planned* should be emphasized; in difficult financial situations, administrators may have to ask faculties to increase class sizes. This would become a matter of changing the plan, and such an adjustment, within reasonable limits, is quite feasible.

Other colleges may have to use different criteria to determine planned capacity. The study leading to this determination can be beneficial in itself since an imbalance may be detected in dormitory and dining hall capacities, classroom seating capacity, and faculty size, all of which should be consistent with the institutional philosophy concerning class size and student/faculty ratios.

The difference in the interpretation of planned capacity is one of the major reasons why the UR cannot be used to compare institutions. A UR of 90 percent at Brunther College is not necessarily better or worse than a UR of 80 percent at some other school. The planned capacity for a school should be a realistic figure based upon the strategies adopted, and it should be viewed as an internal planning device only. A desired UR can then be established, and the actual UR can be evaluated as too high or too low in relation to the desired figure. The numerical value of the UR is less important than its relationship to a desired range and the trend in UR values.

It must be reiterated that the concept of capacity should be viewed as a planned capacity and that it is in no sense a fixed number, because objectives may be adopted to change the capacity, as they were at Brunther College. Another college built new dormitories and then was able to increase its planned capacity, but only because it also had excess classroom space and faculty. Under such strategies,

---

[8] The class schedule at Brunther College requires a full hour of class attendance in each course, which meets three days one week and two days the next and alternates in this manner throughout the semester.

the expenditures would increase the number of required students, but this may be offset by additional capacity and possibly result in no change in the UR. Assume, for instance, that Brunther College hired five new faculty members, increasing expenditures by $100,000 and increasing the net difference (Exhibit IV.5a). If each of these faculty members taught four classes in which maximum enrollment was set at 25, the capacity of the college would increase by:

$$\frac{25 \times 4 \times 5 \text{ teachers}}{5 \text{ (average student course load)}} = 100 \text{ students.}$$

If the increase in faculty occurred in 1969–70, the UR for that year would be (Table IV.2 plus above changes):

$$\frac{\$2,480,000 \text{ (net difference)}}{\$1,370 \text{ (average tuition)}} = 1,810 \text{ students required,}$$

and

$$\frac{1,810 \text{ students required}}{2,125 \text{ new capacity}} = .852 \text{ UR.}$$

The new UR for 1969–70 would be very little different from the previous calculation of .857. The question to be faced by the administrators at this point is whether they can actually obtain the number of students required to compensate for the expenditure. Certainly, private schools need to face the fact that conditions today make strategies for capacity expansion highly questionable.

Analysis of the Utilization Ratio

It should be evident at this point that the utilization ratio is not a measure of a school's financial position. It does not determine the level of either capital or current assets, and it does not determine the amount of the current surplus or deficit. The UR is simply a measure of the ability of an institution to accomplish its mission and is expressed in terms of the degree to which the planned capacity would be utilized at a "break-even" number of students.

The UR will be most effective if a target UR range is established as a planning objective. Establishing such a range provides an effective means for trustees to give general guidance to the president as he attempts to develop long-range plans for the institution. In making this judgment, trustees must consider the institution's resources, the environment, and the other factors of the framework for strategy formulation. The model can serve as a device to assist trustees in communicating their desires to the administration. The administrators would also have a means of relating the faculty's academic programs to the trustees' financial constraints.

To illustrate this process, assume that the trustees of a college were to decide that a UR range of 80–85 percent represented the most effective use of facilities. The total effect of all strategies would be then expected to produce a UR within this desired range. Programs whose academic value had been previously evaluated by the faculty could be submitted to the trustees. If the calculated UR fell within the desired range, the trustees could be reasonably assured that the overall long-range plan was within the resource limitations of the institution.

The lower limit of the UR range (assume 80 percent) might be the level of excess capacity deemed acceptable; it might be the level at which the highest expected tuition rate is reached; or it might represent the trustees' reasonable expectation for maximum non-tuition income. A UR above the desired upper limit (assume 85 percent) might indicate a program that's too expensive for the capacity of the institution, a tuition rate that is too low, or perhaps too many strategic expenditures that are requiring operating income when nontuition income is not available.

Not all schools would establish the same UR target. Institutions with substantial nontuition income may set the target UR at a lower figure. It is even possible for the UR to be zero or even negative. Mathematically, this would happen when the net difference to be paid by tuition is zero or negative. Practically, it can happen when the institution has more nontuition income than operating and capital expenditures. It would be a very rare school that was in this enviable position. This situation could be interpreted to mean that the institution could survive without student tuition, and it also would mean that the school has the option of greater selectivity in accepting students, which is not so rare. It does not necessarily mean that such a school did not charge tuition.

As a planning technique, a UR that is below the target range is not necessarily undesirable. A low UR could mean that the administrators are not planning to do all that the institution's resources will allow them to do; in other words, it implies an ultraconservative financial policy. It can imply a scaling-down of the operation in anticipation of a drop in enrollment. On the other hand, a low UR could also provide the opportunity to lower tuition or to enrich the program through additional strategic expenditures. The UR measures what is financially feasible, not what actually happens. The actual results in comparison with the planned UR may possibly provide a control over expenditures, but at the planning stage the UR only measures what is required to accomplish the long-range plans.

At Brunther College, as well as at several other colleges participating in this study, the idea was expressed that, in order to upgrade or maintain the quality of the student body, they must be in a position to be selective in their admission policy. They felt that financial pressures in the future would make this increasingly difficult. These administrators might determine that they must reduce the UR to a level which required fewer students, allowing themselves the opportunity to accept only the better-qualified applicants without jeopardizing their financial operations.

As has already been pointed out, the administrators seemed to be quite uncertain about the concept of debt capacity. Some acknowledged that they had never considered debt capacity in any objective sense; they simply tried to avoid any long-term debt. The UR can be used to determine the ability to repay debt, but only in conjunction with all other programs and projects planned. If a planned repayment schedule pushes the UR above the target range, it is an immediate signal that other means of financing should be considered or that some strategic expenditure should be dropped from the plans. In establishing the desired level of the UR, administrators must concern themselves with the question of whether the debt level can be maintained with the number of students available.

Earlier in this chapter, the question was raised as to whether Brunther College should have attempted certain strategies for expansion before more definite sources of funds were known. Perhaps it would have been more pertinent to ask when an idea should become a strategy and a part of the long-range financial plan. The most conservative answer for private colleges today is to include only the programs or projects in the long-range plan that can be accomplished within the limits of the target UR, leaving other projects out of the planning process until their source of funds is reasonably assured. This implies a possible and perhaps logical objective of postponing or terminating a program. Two of the test schools in this study had policies of limiting new academic programs to those that replaced existing programs or could be financed from identified sources other than current operating funds. All programs, in other words, were to be self-supporting; no programs were to be undertaken if the original cost or the continuing operating costs would require allocations of resources from operating funds currently or in the foreseeable future. With access to the UR, administrators at these two schools might have avoided the arbitrary application of this policy and could have been more selective in their treatment of academic proposals.

The difficulty of terminating academic programs has already been discussed, but this should not be interpreted to mean that they are never ended. An academic major or department, for instance, can eventually be eliminated through attrition of the faculty members within the department. Under these conditions, it is possible and desirable to separate those costs that will be terminated with the program and show them as a separate expenditure from the on-going strategy of continuing existing programs. As the costs decline or end completely, these can be shown in the schedule of strategic expenditures in the pertinent years, and the effect on the UR can be demonstrated. It would be advisable for administrators to be certain that the faculty agrees with the planned termination of the program.

Most private institutions find that they have more proposed programs and projects than they can afford. They must allocate financial resources to the most appropriate ones. Businesses also face this problem and generally use some measure of ROI as the vehicle for capital allocation. Since profitability is not the objective in private colleges, other means of allocating funds must be determined. Generally, the allocation process in higher education is made initially on academic criteria. The programs with the greatest academic value to the institution presumably are given the highest priority for funds.[9]

One final point must be made about the use of the model. It is not intended to replace the customary operating, capital, and cash budgeting systems. Rather, the model is an instrument designed for use by top administrators who must provide guidance to the lower-level department chairmen and other staff members as they develop the budgets for their responsibility centers. Even though the model may be prepared concurrently with the budgets, the intention is

[9] Even though the UR is intended to measure the financial feasibility of a total package of strategies, it can be helpful in the process of allocating funds. To illustrate, a list of programs could be developed by a faculty group on a subjective basis, ranking them according to academic value. These programs could then be ranked according to the increase in UR required. As the administrators go through the iterative process of trade-offs, they would constantly be asking the question of whether a particular program's academic value justified the increase in the UR. In this manner, faculty members would be involved in the process of allocating funds in that they have made the determination of the rank of projects for which limited funds are available. The target UR established by the trustees would then become the cut-off point in the allocation of funds.

that operating and capital budgets accord with the UR in the planning period under consideration. In this way the UR serves as a control over the budgets submitted by the entire organization. The UR will provide a means for the top administrators and the trustees to evaluate the annual budgets in relation to the total plan of the institution. They will be able to see that the organization is moving in the direction agreed upon when the long-range plan and the UR were set.

EXHIBIT IV.1. Significant characteristics of Brunther College

---

A private, nonprofit college tending toward a miniversity

Affiliation:

Related to the Disciples of Christ Church

Self-perpetuating board of trustees

Assets owned in the name of the trustees

No required number of trustees specified from the denomination

No required number of faculty specified from the denomination

By custom the president and other administrators always from the denomination

Minimal financial support from the denomination

Age: 65 years (founded in 1903)

Location: In mid-Atlantic, industrial city with metropolitan area of approximately 130,000

Closest college: Community college and two women's colleges in the city

Objectives: Progressive, reflecting optimistic view of the future and maximum use of resources

Size (as of 6/30/67):

Students (undergraduate)	1,450–1,500
Faculty	100
Revenue (aux. enterprise, net)	$2.3 million
Assets	8.1 million
Endowment (market)	2.3 million
Plant assets (cost)	5.8 million

Organization:

One school (With 22 academic departments, undergraduate)

One campus

Graduate studies, just beginning

See organization chart (Exhibit II.1)

Growth trends:

Assets growing at rapid rate ($12.0 million by 6/30/69)

Student enrollment increasing about 100 per year

Income exceeded $3.0 million for the year ending 6/30/68

Extensive building program in progress (five buildings under construction in 1968)

Decision-making environment: Administration-oriented; faculty voice becoming stronger but still a responsive one as of 8/1/68

Residence of students: 60% in dormitories; 40% day students

Student background:

From middle ⅓ of high school classes, with perhaps 25% from upper ⅓

From middle-income families

Composition of student body changed from primarily rural to primarily urban in last 3 years

75–80% from home state

EXHIBIT IV.2. Brunther College condensed balance sheet

As of June 30, 1967 (dollars in thousands)	
Assets	
Current fund assets	$ 986.5
Endowment & funds ($2.3 mil. — market value)	1,579.1
Plant assets	5,775.4
Unexpended funds for plant addition	27.9
Agency funds	595.9
Total assets	$8,964.8
Liabilities	
Current liabilities	$ 403.3
Long-term debt	994.0
Total liabilities	$1,397.3
Net book value	7,567.5
Total liabilities & book value	$8,964.8

Statement of current fund operations for the year ended June 30, 1967

Income:		
Student tuition & fees	$1,710.1	
Endowment income	84.9	
Gifts & grants (to current fund only)	132.0	
Government grants	60.1	
Other income	59.7	
Auxiliary enterprise (excess of income over expenses)	236.8	
Total income:		$2,283.6
Expenses:		
Instructional & related activities (salaries & expense)	$1,121.0	
Other administrative & operating expense	829.9	
Total expense:		$1,950.9
Net excess of income over expenses		$ 332.6

EXHIBIT IV.3. Selected financial and enrollment data of Brunther College, 1937–67

(dollars in thousands)

	Regular enroll-ment[a]	Current surplus (deficit)	Income				Endow. assets		Plant assets	Total assets	Total debt
			Tuition	Other	Endow.	Total[b]	Cost	Mkt.			
1966–67	1,389	$332	$1,710	$490	$84	$2,284	$1,579	$2,305	$5,775	$8,963	$1,397
65–66	1,219	300	1,357	343	79	1,779	1,659	2,445	4,992	8,402	1,836
64–65	1,053	197	971	234	74	1,279	1,295	2,200	3,930	6,941	1,268
63–64	766	81	746	184	68	998	1,165	2,076	3,595	5,920	907
62–63	789	103	717	168	69	954	1,030	1,804	3,387	5,465	280
61–62	815	101	655	173	64	892	1,015	1,580	2,596	4,822	388
60–61	747	34	566	125	59	749	992	1,760	2,485	4,260	205
59–60	813	(9)	538	140	59	737	957	1,530	2,416	3,752	16
58–59	782	48	496	114	55	665	936		2,323	3,607	43
57–58	742	54	431	190	55	676	914		1,905	3,288	12
56–57	705	30	366	147	52	565	838		1,653	3,111	5
55–56	692	16	346	64	52	462	740		1,625	2,902	38
54–55	620	29	324	50	52	426	872		1,613	2,872	153
53–54	536	4	275	54	45	374	855		1,323	2,419	59
52–53	498	17	208	51	53	312	482		804	1,748	31
51–52	490	19	196	48	40	284	382		750	1,339	34
50–51	594	(9)	228	37	20	285	346		728	1,263 EST	43
49–50	685	10	267	44	12	323	362		704	1,227	34
48–49	749	26	278	33	14	325	346		679	1,138	40
47–48	696	37	241	30	13	283	346		605	1,062	24
46–47	548	47	167	48	13	229	322		578	989	18

45–46	342	56	94	59	14	167	322	569	953	32
44–45	164	63	48	104	12	158	302	566	917	68
43–44	142	70	52	89	10	132	303	563	906	135
42–43	205	70	47	59	11	127	297	561	931	233
41–42	231	(13)	48	19	10	76	294	555	887	264
40–41	256	(6)	57	10	10	76	289	552	884	251
39–40	261	(15)	55	13	12	80	291	552	876 EST	247
38–39	277	(25)	59	13	10	82	295	550	930	242
37–38	250	(2)	54	25	11	90	295	548	921	208
36–37	218	(16)	46	19	10	74	292	546	930	210

Source: Enrollment data came from catalogs, records of the registrar, and minutes of the meetings of the board of trustees. Financial data was taken from *Report on Examination*, audit reports on Brunther College from 1937–1967, on file in the business office at Brunther College.

a Does not include summer, part-time, or graduate students.

b Includes net income or loss from auxiliary enterprises.

EXHIBIT IV.4. Strategies of Brunther College, August 1, 1968

It is the purpose of Brunther College:

1. To become a regional and residential school, as contrasted with its more local consituency of past years, attracting students from different social, economic, racial, ethnic, and religious environments
2. To accept undergraduate students whose high school performance ranks them in the middle third of their graduating class or above, if they can demonstrate other qualities that indicate potential success in college (This strategy does not diminish the efforts to attract top students as well.)
3. To require a well-rounded core of liberal arts courses of all students regardless of their major field emphases
4. To maintain the moral, ethical, and social standards of a church-related institution
5. To improve the weaker academic departments selectively through significant allocations of resources and to emphasize the academic strengths of the college
6. To improve the general academic program through the addition of high-caliber faculty and the establishment of funded faculty improvement programs
7. To encourage research by members of the faculty and staff who have the interest but at the same time to maintain emphasis on the primary college function of good teaching
8. To offer graduate work at the master's level in the fields where the college has competence and resources
9. To meet the community need for continuing education programs in addition to graduate education when it is compatible with community growth and the college's resources
10. To maintain the size of the undergraduate program between 1,500 and 2,000 students and to allow the graduate division to achieve its greatest foreseeable size
11. To seek actively funds to provide the facilities and other resources required by 1,500–2,000 students (This is manifest in the 10-year development program.)
12. To reorganize the college into three functional areas and within the academic affairs function to constitute 22 departments (see organization chart, Exhibit II.1)
13. To maintain the existing academic areas of study where there is a demand by a significant number of students, recognizing society's changing attitudes about education

---

Note: This statement of strategy was approved by the president of Brunther College.

	Strategies[a]											(Dollars in thousands)	
	(1)	(2)	(3)	(4)	(5)	(6)	(7)	(8)	(9)	(10)	(11)	(13)	Total
Expenditures													
Operating expenses:													
Auxiliary enterprises	$2,281											$2,579	$4,860
All other[b]	99	$384		$120	$65	$175	$211	$251	$185	$352	$75	13,745	15,662
Debt service	1,130		$41							111			1,282
New programs & projects:													
Original cost	1,285		1,192							4,729			7,206
Operating cost	583		93	99	170			206		362			1,513
Total strategic expenditures	$5,378	$384	$1,326	$219	$235	$175	$211	$457	$185	$5,554	$75	$16,324	$30,523
Receipts													
Change in cash balance[c]													—0—
Nontuition receipts:													
Auxiliary enterprises	$3,020											$3,359	$6,379
Endowment income												519	519
Gifts & grants	80		$776				$247			$1,288		1,629	4,020
Other income								$641	$113			950	1,704
Loans received	1,205		415							3,443			5,063
Total nontuition receipts	$4,305		$1,191				$247	$641	$113	$4,731		$6,457	$17,685
Net differences to be paid by student tuition	$1,073	$384	$135	$219	$235	$175	($36)	($184)	$72	$823	$75	$9,867	$12,838

Source: Compiled by researcher from college financial records, adding an 8 percent increase to future expenses.

Note: The figures in this schedule are equal to the sum of the corresponding figures in each of the annual schedules that follow.

[a] Strategy 12 concerning a new organization structure had been accomplished to the point where the strategic expenditure was no longer considered incremental. Consequently, it is omitted from this schedule.

[b] All other expenses represent the sum of the expenses for all responsibility centers identified for the institution.

[c] In this research, cash balances were held constant for convenience. This is neither necessary nor realistic in practice. An excessive cash balance can be a source of funds, and a deficient balance can require debt financing. If the UR is to measure debt requirements, it will be necessary to include changes in cash balances.

EXHIBIT IV.5b. Brunther College annual schedules of strategic expenditures

Proposed for the year 1968–69
(Dollars in thousands)

							Strategies						
	(1)	(2)	(3)	(4)	(5)	(6)	(7)	(8)	(9)	(10)	(11)	(13)	Total
Expenditures													
Operating expenses:													
Auxiliary enterprises	$391											$ 437	$ 828
All other	17	$65		$20	$11	$30	$36	$43	$31	$ 60	$13	2,344	2,670
Debt service	202												202
New programs & projects:													
Original cost										3,777			3,777
Operating cost	75			17	29			8		12			141
Total strategic expenditures	$685	$65	–0–	$37	$40	$30	$36	$51	$31	$3,849	$13	$2,781	$7,618
Receipts													
Change in cash balance													–0–
Nontuition receipts													
Auxiliary enterprises	$533											$ 571	1,104
Endowment income												88	88
Gifts & grants							$41			$ 711		279	1,031
Other income								$90	$19			162	271
Loans received										3,067			3,067
Total nontuition receipts	$533						$41	$90	$19	$3,778		$1,100	$5,561
Net difference to be paid by student tuition	$152	$65	–0–	$37	$40	$30	($ 5)	($39)	$12	$ 71	$13	$1,681	$2,057

Proposed for the year 1969–70
(Dollars in thousands)

Strategies

	(1)	(2)	(3)	(4)	(5)	(6)	(7)	(8)	(9)	(10)	(11)	(13)	Total
Expenditures													
Operating expenses:													
Auxiliary enterprises	$420											$ 475	$ 895
All other	18	$71		$22	$12	$32	$39	$ 46	$34	$ 65	$14	2,533	2,886
Debt service	202									27			229
New programs & projects:													
Original cost										952			952
Operating cost	82			18	31			19		77			227
Total strategic expenditures	$722	$71	–0–	$40	$43	$32	$39	$ 65	$34	$1,121	$14	$3,008	$5,189
Receipts													
Change in cash balance													–0–
Nontuition receipts:													
Auxiliary enterprises	$506											$ 611	$1,117
Endowment income												96	96
Gifts & grants							$44			$ 577		301	922
Other income								$102	$21			175	298
Loans received										376			376
Total nontuition receipts	$506		–0–				$44	$102	$21	$ 953		$1,183	$2,809
Net difference to be paid by student tuition	$216	$71	–0–	$40	$43	$32	($ 5)	($ 37)	$13	$ 168	$14	$1,825	$2,380

EXHIBIT IV. 5b (continued)

Proposed for the year 1970–71
(Dollars in thousands)

					Strategies								
	(1)	(2)	(3)	(4)	(5)	(6)	(7)	(8)	(9)	(10)	(11)	(13)	Total
Expenditures													
Operating expenses:													
Auxiliary enterprises	$ 453											$ 513	$ 966
All other	20	$76		$24	$13	$35	$42	$ 50	$37	$ 70	$15	2,730	3,112
Debt service	242		$ 14							28			284
New programs & projects:													
Original cost	1,285		1,192										2,477
Operating cost	131		29	20	34			25		84			323
Total strategic expenditures	$2,131	$76	$1,235	$44	$47	$35	$42	$ 75	$37	$182	$15	$3,243	$7,162
Receipts													
Change in cash balance													–0–
Nontuition receipts:													
Auxiliary enterprises	$ 652											715	$1,367
Endowment income												103	103
Gifts & grants	80		$ 776				$49					324	1,229
Other income								$117	$23			189	329
Loans received	$1,205		415										1,620
Total nontuition receipts	$1,937		$1,191				$49	$117	$23			$1,331	$4,648
Net difference to be paid by student tuition	194	$76	44	$44	$47	$35	($ 7)	($ 42)	$14	$182	$15	$1,912	$2,514

Proposed for the year 1971–72
(Dollars in thousands)

Strategies

	(1)	(2)	(3)	(4)	(5)	(6)	(7)	(8)	(9)	(10)	(11)	(13)	Total
Expenditures													
Operating expenses:													
Auxiliary enterprises	$489											$ 555	$1,044
All other	21	$83		$26	$14	$37	$45	$ 54	$40	$ 76	$16	2,950	3,362
Debt service	242		$13							28			283
New programs & projects:													
Original cost													–0–
Operating cost	142		31	21	37			73		91			395
Total strategic expenditures	$894	$83	$44	$47	$51	$37	$45	$127	$40	$195	$16	$3,505	$5,084
Receipts													
Change in cash balance													–0–
Nontuition receipts:													
Auxiliary enterprises	$664											721	1,385
Endowment income												112	112
Gifts & grants							$54					349	403
Other income								$153	$24			204	381
Loans received													–0–
Total nontuition receipts	$664						$54	$153	$24			$1,386	$2,281
Net difference to be paid by student tuition	$230	$83	$44	$47	$51	$37	($ 9)	($ 26)	$16	$195	$16	$2,119	$2,803

EXHIBIT IV. 5b (continued)

Proposed for the year 1972–73
(Dollars in thousands)

						Strategies							
	(1)	(2)	(3)	(4)	(5)	(6)	(7)	(8)	(9)	(10)	(11)	(13)	Total
Expenditures													
Operating expenses:													
Auxiliary enterprises	$528											$ 599	$1,127
All other	23	$89		$28	$15	$41	$49	$ 58	$43	$ 81	$17	3,188	3,632
Debt service	242		$14							28			284
New programs & projects:													
Original cost													–0–
Operating cost	153		33	23	39			81		98			427
Total strategic expenditures	$946	$89	$47	$51	$54	$41	$49	$139	$43	$207	$17	$3,787	$5,470
Receipts													
Change in cash balance													–0–
Nontuition receipts:													
Auxiliary enterprises	$665											$ 741	$1,406
Endowment income												120	120
Gifts & grants							$59					376	435
Other income								$179	$26			220	425
Loans received													–0–
Total nontuition receipts	$665						$59	$179	$26			$1,457	$2,386
Net difference to be paid by student tuition	$281	$89	$47	$51	$54	$41	($10)	($ 40)	$17	$207	$17	$2,330	$3,084

EXHIBIT IV.6. Computation of student capacity at Brunther College

	Maximum enrollment in all courses[a]	Aver. no. of courses per student	Maximum student capacity col. (1)/col. (2)
Fall 1967	10,153	5	2,030
Spring 1968	10,281	5	2,055
Fall 1968	9,952	5	1,990
Total capacity (3 semesters)			6,075
Average student capacity (6,075/3)			2,025

[a] The figures were taken from the class schedules for these three semesters, records of which are on file in the registrar's office at Brunther College.

CHAPTER V

The Test of the Usefulness of the Model

THE ultimate value of this or any other financial planning model can only be determined through application in a variety of situations. Its real value as an information system must be determined by the users, college presidents and their administrators. Consequently, the three stages of the model were implemented at Brunther College to test its value empirically. This was done first in a simulated session with top administrators; later work was undertaken to adopt the system there. The model was further tested at four other private institutions. The schools varied in characteristics; each was selected to answer particular questions coming out of the work at Brunther College.

The Test at Brunther College

At Brunther College the model was presented for the first time at a meeting of top administrators, including the president. The utilization ratio received particular attention. Each of the men present had been interviewed individually in the initial compilation of strategies. One purpose of this meeting was to determine exceptions or additions to the list that might develop during interchange among the group.

In the early fall each year Brunther College had to decide the tuition rate to charge for the coming year. This was an issue at the time of the meeting. Although not the express purpose of the meeting, it was expected that alternative trade-offs between tuition, number of students required, strategic expenditures, and time could be analyzed with the model. However, the newness of its concepts limited the degree to which the administrators were willing to rely upon the model in a single session. In addition, much of the time in the meeting was taken up in explaining the concepts to the participants. This, too, was a purpose of the meeting.

The discussion of strategy tended to substantiate the list in Exhibit IV.4, but the dean did express concern about strategy 2, which implied that admission standards were to be aimed lower than the top high school students. He did agree that the current policy was to accept average students as well as the top high school graduates. The director of institutional research was concerned with Brunther's strategy to become a regional and residential school; however, he agreed that at present the college was operating under this strategy.

In view of the projected rising UR (Table IV.2), more discussion was expected on strategy 10, attempting to maintain the size of the college between 1,500 and 2,000 students. The significance of the UR was not explained until after the discussion of strategies, but even then very little concern was expressed about the college's ability to maintain the parameters of enrollment set in the strategy. The 1,500–2,000 level apparently was set with the rationalized belief that it was a maximum. The strategy should perhaps more appropriately state that the college intended to maintain enrollment at a minimum level with sufficient growth to allow innovation in program and stability in financial condition.

Several points were made about the effects of the environment. By constructing dormitories, a student center, and other major buildings, Brunther College may have forced itself into a position of requiring larger numbers of students or other sources of revenue than were available. The trend at the college toward greater cultivation of the federal agencies may ultimately affect the college's private status. In the background of every strategy discussion was the widening gap between private school tuition and the charges by state-supported institutions. This accented the need for long-range planning.

Although the participants were able to see that the rising UR was an undesirable situation for Brunther College, there was no target UR to use for comparison. The participants realized at the meeting that the board of trustees had not yet established such a target UR. Had the participants been given a desired range, they might have felt more pressure to make concrete proposals for improvements of the UR. A range for the UR which both the trustees and the administration agreed upon would provide a common goal for the institution's financial programs in much the same way as an agreed-upon rate of ROI does for the business firm.

At Brunther College only 15 percent of the income was derived from endowment income, gifts and grants, and other outside sources (Table II.2 and Exhibit IV.2). There was no wealthy constituency from which to expect major contributions; consequently, the burden of financial support was on the students themselves. Strategic expenditure commitments were therefore limited to the combination of the number of students enrolled multiplied by the tuition, room, and board rates. To commit expenditures beyond this source of revenue requires borrowed funds and invites substantial risk.

Of particular interest was the value of the UR in helping to formulate alternatives for the 1969–70 tuition rate. The alternative of leaving the tuition rate at existing levels was weighed against the number of students required and against various trade-offs of strategic expenditures. The final rate was not set at the meeting, but the issues discussed to test the UR did provide additional insight into the alternatives available.

To a great extent the eventual usefulness of the UR as a quantitative instrument will depend upon the willingness of administrators to apply it. At Brunther College about 85 percent of the current fund income has historically come from student charges. Because of this high percentage, any plan for new projects or changes in existing programs must be evaluated in terms of the number of students that can be expected. This fact makes the UR a valid measure of the financial feasibility at Brunther College since the UR is expressly intended to relate strategic expenditures to students required.

The Brunther College experience did raise a question that had to be answered in the tests at the other colleges and universities. Could the UR be used in schools where the proportion of revenue received from students was less than at Brunther College? The work at the test schools was structured largely to confront this question.

The group achieved sufficient understanding of the UR to suggest various program changes and to test their effect on the UR. From this exercise the level of confidence rose significantly, and the desire to put the model into actual use was initiated. Table V.1 illustrates some of the conditions tested, and Table V.2 demonstrates their effect on the UR.

Conclusions from the Test

Several conclusions can be drawn from the experience in the planning meeting.

1. The three-stage financial planning model is more than just a logical way of classifying accounts for recording purposes; it is a planning device that makes analysis and decision making more effective. Its three stages are

    a. strategy formulation using the framework to guide in considering all factors,

TABLE V.1. Alternatives suggested in order to change the utilization ratio at Brunther College

	Increase (decrease) in net difference
1. Increase in endowment of $1.0 million: would increase endowment income by about	($ 50,000)
2. Increase federal grants (specific proposals were already placed with federal agencies, and it was assumed that these could be used for current operations)	($100,000)
3. Increase size of certain classes when space was available in the new fine arts building: expected to save 3–4 teachers	($ 50,000)
4. Not building the student activity center: alternative no longer available	–o–
5. Increase tuition: would not change the net difference but would result in the need for fewer students, which is accounted for in the UR by dividing the net difference by a larger tuition rate	–o–
6. Idle capacity might develop in the dormitories of 100 beds: would result in an increase in the net difference by approximately $320 per vacant bed, or	$ 32,000
Change in net difference resulting from the meeting	($168,000)

    b. identification of strategic expenditures with strategies, and

    c. computation and manipulation of the UR.

2. The UR showed the possibility of becoming a common denominator to guide the planning process in a concise manner which is not available in the typical voluminous long-range budgets.

3. The UR served as a guide in relating costs of programs and projects to available resources and in this respect served much the same function as the ROI analysis does for industry.

4. The UR can be valuable in converting broad strategy statements into tangible tools of analysis.

5. There is a need for strategies concerning the source of resources as well as the allocation of resources through strategic expenditures.

6. There is a need to develop a target UR, to be approved by the trustees, which will guide administrators as they design a workable set of strategies for both resource determination and allocation.

TABLE V.2. Effect of suggested alternatives on the utilization ratio at Brunther College

Year	Net difference (from Exhibit IV.5b)	Proposed decrease (from Table V.1)	Adjusted net difference	New aver. tuition	SR/SC[a]	UR
	(in 1000's)	(in 1000's)	(in 1000's)			
1968–69	$2,057	–0–[b]	$2,057	$1,340	1,535/2,025	.758
1969–70	2,380	($168)	2,212	1,420[c]	1,551/2,025	.765
1970–71	2,514	(168)	2,346	1,440	1,629/2,025	.805
1971–72	2,803	(168)	2,635	1,450	1,817/2,025	.897
1972–73	3,084	(168)	2,916	1,450	2,011/2,025	.993

[a] SR/SC: the students required divided by the student capacity.
[b] At the time of the meeting the 1968–69 budget had already been approved by the trustees.
[c] A $50 average increase in tuition would result from a $100 increase in the tuition of the entering class. The $100 increase would be applied to each entering class for four years until all students were paying the higher rate.

7. The model must be tested in institutions with larger sources of endowment and gift and grant income than Brunther College has.

Test of the General Applicability to Other Schools

The model clearly emphasizes enrollment and the fact that there is probably some optimum student body size. As the model was applied to more and more situations in the test schools with characteristics different from those of Brunther College[1] and, later, in other applications, it became more apparent that the UR should be in the range of 80–90 percent. To plan for it to be less than this might indicate several conditions: the realization that enrollments would not be as high as was desired and that plans should not be made which overextended the institutions; a program that was too rich in any number of ways; or that the institution had substantial nontuition income (and perhaps that it was not doing all that it was capable of).

Whenever the UR exceeded 90 percent, it was usually found that some area of the program was overextended. The point was made earlier that if the students, faculty, and other resources of all departmental programs balanced perfectly, it would be theoretically possible to maintain a UR of 100 percent. Since this is seldom the case, the more popular programs are usually undermanned and underfinanced, while other departments may at least have too large a faculty. This condition became a deterrent when the UR tended to exceed 90 percent. Also, when funds are diverted to non-academic use or even to applications slightly remote from the academic program, the UR will tend to rise. For this reason, schools such as Brunther College should resist their endeavors. Although the role of higher education in general may include teaching, research, and public service, each institution must determine what its share of the burden is to be. The decision for private colleges most often will be based on financial criteria stemming from the level of enrollment.

At the four test schools, the results varied; in most instances the model was equally as applicable as at Brunther College but the schools' different characteristics tended either to restrict the need for the model or to suggest further study.

---

[1] The general characteristics of the test schools are described in Exhibits V.1 through V.4 at the end of this chapter.

In testing the model at these schools, it was not intended to determine the specific effect that each of the many characteristics of the schools would have on the model. Nor was it intended to evaluate or criticize the strategies of these schools. The only purpose was to determine if the applicability of the model in private schools would be destroyed by the presence of different institutional and organizational characteristics. The schools chosen differed from Brunther in age, size, organizational complexity, growth trends, endowment size, geographic location, major sources of income, church affiliation, institutional objectives, and administrative competence and attitude.

The age of the schools had only indirect significance to the proposed model. The older schools had had longer to generate alumni with the financial ability to make major contributions to the school, but this characteristic was evaluated more directly in the consideration of major sources of income and endowment size. These latter two characteristics had an effect on the numerical value of the UR, but they did not limit the methodology of the proposed model.

Church affiliation had no effect on the model since the churches exercised little or no direct control over the institutions; it did, however, present an additional source of outside income. It was also one of the environmental factors to be considered as part of the framework for strategy formulation, but it did not deter the use of the model.

Growth trends, institutional objectives, and administrative competence and attitudes all have a profound effect on the strategies adopted by the institution and should be considered in making the strategy framework analysis, but again they did not seem to limit the applicability of the model. To some extent these factors contributed to the value of the model in that each could be objectively evaluated as part of the strategy analysis and clearer statements concerning these characteristics could be developed.

Of all the characteristics listed, only size and organizational complexity at the large university seemed to have a significant effect on the methodology required by the model.

Student capacity, needed for the UR computation, was found to be constrained by a number of different factors. At one of the smaller residential schools it was dormitory capacity, since the rural setting did not offer other types of housing. At miniversity B capacity was recognized to be considerably higher than actual enrollment since there was both excess dormitory and class space; in addition, faculty loads were not large. Here the desire to maintain small classes was the limiting factor on capacity. At the well-endowed college great emphasis was placed on having small classes and having adequate contact between students and professors on a one-to-one basis. This limited the plans about capacity here too. At the large university student capacity was not easily measurable in any terms. There had been some attempts at a mechanical count of classroom seats with the idea that this should be balanced with dormitory and dining hall space, faculty size and loads, and student service facilities and staff. Although all these matters were under consideration, very little had been done to reach a conclusion.

As mentioned before, two of the schools had a policy that no new academic programs were to be initiated unless they were self-supporting or were replacements for existing offerings. This policy is frequently employed in private colleges and usually is the result of past financial difficulties. Both of the schools had plans for various capital additions and even major program changes such as a school for international studies, but these were expected to be self-supporting and even to allow for greater enrollment (capacity). In light of these policies, it is interesting to note the resulting URs. At the small residential college the UR rises constantly throughout the five-year planning period, for several reasons: rising price levels, increased costs of operating and maintaining the new facilities, and a need to reduce faculty in several areas (Table V.3). The UR at

TABLE V.3. Computation of utilization ratio for 1968–73 at small college

Year	Net difference (in 1000's)	Tuition rate[a]	SR/SC	UR
1968–69	$ 1,936	$1,615	1,199/1,800	.67
1969–70	2,018	1,715	1,177/1,800	.65
1970–71	2,218	1,715	1,293/1,800	.72
1971–72	2,441	1,715	1,423/1,800	.79
1972–73	2,689	1,715	1,568/1,800	.87
Total	$11,302			

[a] The tuition rate is the planned charge for the five-year period. The increase in 1969–70 will be to all students, not just the entering class as is the practice at Brunther College.

miniversity B rises at first and then falls significantly (Table V.4). The planning period was longer at this institution because it had been involved in an earlier ten-year planning process, which indicated that a five-year period was not enough. For the purpose of

TABLE V.4. Computation of utilization ratio for the years ended 6/30/69 through 6/30/76 at miniversity B

Year	Total strategic expenditures	Nontuition income	Net difference	Tuition rate	SR/SC	UR
1968–69	$ 6,254	$ 3,000	$ 3,254	$1,400	2,323/2,400	.97
1969–70	5,076	3,031	2,045	1,400	1,461/2,400	.61
1970–71	6,080	3,075	3,005	1,400	2,146/2,400	.89
1971–72	7,030	3,190	3,840	1,400	2,743/2,400	1.14
1972–73	6,240	2,795	3,445	1,400	2,460/2,400	1.03
1973–74	6,740	3,955	2,785	1,600	1,740/2,400	.73
1974–75	6,860	3,940	2,920	1,600	1,825/2,400	.76
1975–76	6,130	3,945	2,185	1,600	1,365/2,400	.57
Total	$50,410	$26,931	$23,479			

this study, only eight years were illustrated since the trend beyond that period was the same. In the fourth and fifth years the UR, in excess of 100 percent, indicates a potential deficit unless adjustments are made. In fact, there was a deficit in the first year with the UR at 97 percent. Because plans become more nebulous and uncertain as they are extended into the future, administrators and others tend all too often to project results more from rationalization than from analysis. Results in later years may be projected to justify whatever one wants to do. There is reason to think this type of planning may have been the case at miniversity B. The application of the model was not restricted at either institution, however, and perhaps was helpful in demonstrating the weaknesses in plans.

The general questions to be answered at the well-endowed college were:

1. To what extent was the applicability of the model affected by substantially larger sources of nontuition income?
2. Did any other noticeable characteristics limit the applicability of the model?
3. What were the considerations in planned capacity here?

The greater sources of nontuition income along with a stable program tended to relieve the pressure for higher tuition and for more students, at least in comparison with the three other small schools. So long as the sources of outside revenue are sufficient and no major changes in objectives are anticipated, the need for the UR or for any other quantitative measure is reduced. However, one of the concerns was whether the outside source of income would continue, together with the fact that there had been a decline in applicants for admission.

As the administrators observed the uncertainties in these two trends, they could have obtained valuable information from the UR, even though financial resources were ample at that time. In effect, this affluent school had been able to offset rising costs with nontuition income, so that student tuition was only required to pay 45–50 percent of the total operating costs. They intended to try to increase nontuition income in the future in order to continue the proportion of tuition income at 50 percent or less. By increasing nontuition income and maintaining a relatively stable academic program, they expected to keep tuition rate increases to a minimum. These expectations concerning nontuition income and operating cost affected the emphasis placed upon the UR; a school that expects nontuition income to increase faster than costs will feel less pressure for more students or higher tuition rates, and the administrators will have little interest in a quantitative measure such as the UR. This condition is, of course, contradictory to financial conditions at most private institutions, where the pressure on tuition income can be expected to continue and to increase.

The stability of the academic program objectives at this well-endowed school also tends to reduce the applicability of the model, which places emphasis on the financial effects of changes in strategies. If a college or university anticipates few incremental strategies, the need for the model is greatly reduced. Such a school nevertheless does face two problems. First, they must be certain that evolutionary change in the program will allow them to keep pace with the changing demand for education. And second, they must assure themselves that the rising costs of even the existing program can be covered by existing sources of income. The analysis called for in the first stage of the model will be helpful in approaching the first problem, and the UR could be used to provide the necessary assurance in the second situation; however, little new information would be made available through use of the UR.

The stable program and a nontuition income increasing at least at the same pace as operating costs could make the numerical values of the UR lower than at the other small schools. However, the UR, of course, depends on the value assigned to planned capacity, the formula's denominator, and here the concept of capacity was defined in such a way as to make the numerical values of the UR reasonably close to those at the other schools (Table V.5). Capacity was generally constrained by the size of the faculty and by the desire for small classes with as much personal contact between faculty and students as possible. Dormitory space was not a constraint since traditionally students had lived in the adjacent town.

At the large university the research tested only the effects of larger size and more complex organizational relationships on the methodology proposed in this study. In particular, it was felt that the range of size of the other schools participating in this study was not large enough to provide a good comparison of private schools' administration of strategic expenditures with industry's methods of managing capital expenditures.

Strategies were not identified here as was done at other schools. The substantially greater resources allowed this university to adopt objectives in teaching, research, and public service, three clearly separate functional areas with strategies that were only remotely related to each other. To list the strategies would have required the efforts of one group of administrators for the university and another group for the hospital; according to one administrator, it was doubtful that any one individual other than the president

TABLE V.5. Computation of the utilization ratio for the planning period 7/1/68 through 6/30/73 at well-endowed college

Year	Strategic expenditures (in 1000's)	Nontuition income (in 1000's)	Net difference (in 1000's)	Average tuition rate	SR/SC	UR
1968–69	$ 4,238	$ 1,880	$ 2,358	$1,600	1,473/2,000	.736
1969–70	4,662	1,963	2,699	1,700	1,588/2,000	.794
1970–71	6,878	3,848	3,030	1,825	1,660/2,000	.830
1971–72	10,792	7,435	3,357	1,950	1,721/2,000	.860
1972–73	12,506	8,782	3,724	2,025	1,839/2,000	.920
Total	$39,076	$23,908	$15,168			

could speak for both. In addition, some faculty members of the university as well as the hospital were involved only in research and did no teaching.

Without identifying strategies it was not possible to accumulate strategic expenditures. This step could be performed, but first it would be necessary to exclude the university's hospital, for in the next step, calculating the UR, the hospital must be excluded. The UR is a ratio of students required to students at capacity, neither of which have relevance in a hospital. For this reason, other measures should be developed to analyze the hospital expenditures.

If it is possible to eliminate the hospital by clearly separating its income and expenses from those of the university, then theoretically it would be possible to apply the UR to the university only. Such a separation requires an allocation of expenses for shared resources and services that is not customary in higher education, although the separation of divisions in large multidivision companies such as Dupont, General Electric, and General Motors demonstrates that it is not impossible. It would require a more elaborate accounting system, which was in the process of being developed at this university.

This university had large sources of outside income; would the UR be useful to such an institution? Only 14 percent of the university's income was derived from student tuition and fees (Table V.6). It was thus far less reliant upon income from students for financial stability than were the smaller schools.

TABLE V.6. Percentage of total income coming from tuition at the five institutions

Brunther College	75%
Small college	75%
Miniversity B	62%
Well-endowed college	47%
Large university	14%

Less stability in the educational program was observed here than at the smaller schools. For instance, the university had recently instituted a major in computer science, approved a graduate school of business administration, and substantially revised the undergraduate curriculum. To assure that the additional costs of such changes do not exceed the sources of income requires constant scrutiny, which a measure such as the UR could make possible.

There is evidence that even the wealthy institutions such as the large university and the well-endowed college rely on students for the constant flow of income for their operations. As the pressure on private education continues to mount, there will be a need for objective information concerning the trends in this flow. The UR can be used for this purpose. Administrators of a large university should wait until they have set up the required separate accounting systems before applying the UR, but there is no reason why they cannot use the first two stages of the proposed model immediately. The university's broad missions could be broken into viable strategies, and strategic expenditures could be identified with strategies. These two steps would provide useful information to administrators; the model, of course, would remain incomplete without the third step, the computation of the UR.

One further comment is necessary on the influence of size on the construction of the model. Larger institutions have greater influence with federal authorities who dispense research contracts, grants, and loans, and they are also more likely to have renowned faculty members who can attract funds in their own name and who will also attract students, particularly at the graduate level. Size itself thus becomes a resource of great value in attracting other resources, but it is also a difficult consideration to pinpoint. Both the size and the organizational complexity of a large university create difficulties for the development of the model that have not yet been studied. For this reason, its application to the large university should await further research.

Finally, a word should be said about the relationship of the model to academic excellence in programs. Certainly, many of the abstract values of academic programs are not to be measured by the proposed model. It is only a financial planning model intended to measure the financial ability of an institution to accomplish its strategies. Quality academic programs often are the result of such factors as higher faculty salaries, more faculty research, selective admission standards, and emphasis on faculty education and development. All of these factors have financial implications that can be compared to financial constraints through the use of the UR. Indications of the value of academic programs, the competence of the faculty, and the quality of the student body are often estimated by other measures such as the percentage of graduates applying to graduate schools, scores on various achievement tests, and by the number of terminal degree holders on the faculty. These are all worthwhile tools, but they measure values outside the scope of this study. The model proposed here only measures the institution's financial ability to sustain the high standards of quality.

EXHIBIT V.1. Significant characteristics of small college

A private, nonprofit College

Affiliation:
  Related to United Methodist Church
  Self-perpetuating board of trustees
  Assets owned in the name of the trustees
  No required number of trustees specified from the denomination
  No required number of faculty specified from the denomination
  Present president and other administrators not from the denomination
  Minimal financial support from the denomination

Age: 118 years (founded in 1850)

Location: In rural region the state; ⅓ of state's population is within 50-mile
  radius

Closest college: Large state university 18 miles from campus, with several others
  including community colleges within 40 miles

Objectives: To remain a small liberal arts college with evolutionary change in
  academic programs

Size (as of 6/30/67):
Students	1,100
Faculty	80
Revenue (aux. enterprises, net)	$ 2.5 million
Assets	$13.9 million
Endowment (market)	$ 6.7 million
Plant assets (cost)	$ 7.0 million

Organization:
  One school (with 19 undergraduate academic departments)
  One campus plus a biological station
  No graduate program

Growth trends:
  Steady growth in number of students reflecting the national trend
  Little increase in faculty and facilities

Decision-making environment:
  Unsettled, historically faculty-oriented
  New president creating tendency toward administration-orientation but with
    resistance

Residence of students: 90% in dormitories; 10% day students

Student background:
  From upper and middle ⅓ of high school classes, tending toward the middle
  From middle-income families
  Urban home state predominant background with a small minority from sur-
    rounding states

EXHIBIT V.2. Significant characteristics of miniversity B

A private, nonprofit miniversity tending toward a university

Affiliation:
Southern Baptist Convention
Self-perpetuating board of trustees with no limitation of term of office
Assets owned in the name of trustees
¾ of board must be Baptist (not necessarily home-state Baptist)
President must be Baptist (most other administrators were also Baptist although no specific requirement)
No required number of faculty specified from the denomination (about 40% were Baptist)
Substantial financial support: $300,000 (approx.) per year plus a significant number of students

Age: 85 years (founded in 1883)

Location: Central southeast rural town; area population about 25,000

Closest college: Private and state schools within 25 miles

Objectives: To remain with existing curricula with greater involvement in social and international problems of the day

Size (as of 6/31/67):

Students	2,100
Faculty	116
Revenue (excl. aux. enterprises)	$ 3.9 million
Assets	$20.3 million
Endowment (market)	$ 4.9 million
Plant Assets (cost)	$15.4 million

Organization:
Four schools (liberal arts, music, bus. adm. and law) —approx. 24 departments
Two campuses (200 miles apart)
Several graduate offerings

Growth trends: Minimal in students, faculty, and assets

Decision-making environment: Historically "faculty-oriented" but evidence of change with a new administration

Residence of students: 95% in dormitories; 5% day students

Student background:
Upper and middle ⅓ of high school classes
From middle-income families
From both urban and rural families of the South
70% from home state

EXHIBIT V.3. Significant characteristics of well-endowed college

A private, nonprofit miniversity

Affiliation: None

Age: 219 years (founded in 1749)

Location: In mid-Atlantic small town with little industry; no adjacent large cities

Closest college: Within 50-mile radius—a large state university and other private schools

Objectives: To retain liberal arts undergraduate curriculum and law school

Size (as of 6/30/67):

Students	1,300–1,400
Faculty	135
Revenue (excl. aux. enterprises)	$ 3.9 million
Assets	$32.9 million
Endowment (market)	$20.5 million
Plant Assets (cost)	$12.1 million

Organization:
   Three schools (with 26 academic departments)
   One campus
   Law school–only graduate program

Growth trends:
   2% per year growth in student size expected
   Selective replacement of older buildings but no additional investment other than replacement
   Endowment expected to be increased by an amount equal to increase in plant assets

Decision-making environment:
   Faculty is strong, almost solely responsible for the academic program
   Faculty also influential in admission, faculty additions, design of buildings, and other administrative affairs

Residence of students: 45% in dormitories; 50–55% off-campus residential; perhaps 2% day students

Student background:
   From top 10–20% of high school and preparatory school classes
   From upper-income families predominately, significant number of professional parents
   Urban with a wide national distribution; minority from home state

EXHIBIT V.4. Significant characteristics of large university

A private, nonprofit university

Affiliation: Presbyterian Church

Age: 129 years (founded in 1839)

Location: Northeast; medium-sized city in heavy industrial region; several state and private institutions within 50-mile radius

Objective: To be a top-quality, national, private university

Size (as of October 1968):

Students	7,500 approx.
Faculty	900 approx.
Revenue	$ 40.0 million approx.
Assets	$200.0 million approx.
Endowment	$ 65.0 million approx.
Plant Assets	$125.0 million approx.

Organization:
Nine schools (in excess of 40 academic departments
One campus (plus a marine laboratory)
Large hospital facility
Undergraduate and several professional degrees offered

Growth trend: Selective growth in student body within the parameters set by existing high standards for admission

Decision-making environment: Academic departments have strong voice in their programs, in budget matters, admissions, capital expenditures, tenure, and related matters

Residence of students: 90% in dormitories

Student background:
National distribution
High scholastic achievement
Mostly from urban areas
From middle- and upper-income families primarily
Only 20% from home state

Appendix

Bibliography

Formulas for Quantitative Measure of Effectiveness of Strategic Expenditures

To determine surplus (or deficit) from income-producing auxiliary enterprises (variables are identified below):

If $RD \leq CD$, $RH \leq CH$, and/or $SR \leq SC$ (operating below capacity):

$$[RD(LD) - OD] + [RH(BH) - OH] + [SR(RB - OB)] = S.$$

If $RD > CD$, $RH > CH$, and/or $SR > SC$ (operating above capacity):

$$[CD(LD) - OD] + [CH(BH) - OH] + [SC(RB - OB)] = S.$$

To determine nontuition income:

$$ER + GG + GF + LR + OR = NT.$$

To determine the surplus (or deficit) from each of the auxiliary enterprises separately, the following equations might be used:

If $RD < CD$, then,

$$RD(LD) - (OD)(1 + r)^t = S_1,$$

or

if $RD > CD$, then,

$$CD(LD) - (OD)(1 + r)^t = S_1.$$

If $RH < CH$, then,

$$RH(BH) - (OH)(1 + r)^t = S_2,$$

or

if $RH > CH$, then,

$$CH(BH) - (OH)(1 + r)^t = S_2.$$

If $SR < SC$, then,

$$SR(RB - OB)(1 + r)^t = S_3,$$

or

if $SR > SC$, then,

$$SC(RB - OB)(1 + r)^t = S_3.$$

Since some institutions may have other auxiliary enterprise income, the general formula for total surplus (or deficit) from auxiliary enterprises for a given institution will then be:

$$S_1 + S_2 + S_3 + \cdots + S_n = S.$$

Before the basic formula can be developed, one additional equation is necessary to reflect all sources of revenue and borrowing other than tuition received from students:

$$ER + GG + GF + OR + LR = NT.$$

All factors in this equation were derived exogenously to the model, but this is not necessary in every case; for instance, endowment income (*ER*) could be derived. The erratic pattern of change in these amounts make it difficult to develop a reliable method of computing them. For this reason, it was felt that they should be obtained from estimates made for empirical data. With these supporting equations determined, the basic formula for the utilization ratio is:

$$\frac{(OI)(1+r)^t - NT + AR - S}{TR} \times \frac{1}{SC} = UR.$$

RD	students required in dormitories
CD	students capacity of dormitories
OD	operating costs of dormitories (as defined by each institution)
LD	room rent per student
S	excess of dormitory rent over operating costs (may be negative)

RH	students required in dining halls
CH	student capacity of dining halls
OH	operating costs of dining halls (as defined by each institution)
BH	board charge per student
S	excess of board charge over operating costs (may be negative)

RB	bookstore receipts per student (average)
OB	operating costs of bookstore per student (average)

SR	institution's student requirements (total enrollment)
SC	institution's classroom capacity (as defined for planning purposes)

OI	institution's operating cost, other than in OD, OH, or OB
AR	annual costs of asset replacement and debt curtailment from undesignated funds

ER	endowment income
GG	private gifts and grants
GF	federal gifts and grants
OR	other receipts
LR	loans received
NT	total nonstudent income (*ER, GG, GF, OR,* and *LR*)

TR	tuition rate per student
UR	Utilization Ratio (will be the resulting output)

r	average rate of increase (decrease) in operating expenditures
t	number of planning periods from the current year

Bibliography

A. Higher Education Sources

1. Books

American Council on Education. *College and University Business Administration.* Vols. I-III. Washington, D.C., 1952, 1955, 1968.

——. *Needed Expansion of Facilities for Higher Education, 1958–1970, How Much Will It Cost?* Washington, D.C., 1958.

Bowen, Howard R. *The Finance of Higher Education.* Berkeley, Calif.: Carnegie Commission on Higher Education, 1968.

Bowen, William G. *The Economics of the Major Private Universities.* Berkeley, Calif.: Carnegie Commission of Higher Education, 1968.

Burns, Gerald P. *Trustees in Higher Education.* New York: Independent College Funds of America, 1966.

Callahan, Raymond E. *Education and the Cult of Efficiency.* Chicago: University of Chicago Press, 1962.

Conant, James B. *The Citadel of Learning.* New Haven: Yale University Press, 1956.

Dobbins, Charles G., and Calvin B. T. Lee (eds.). *Whose Goals for American Higher Education.* Washington, D.C.: American Council on Education, 1968.

Dressel, Paul L. *The Undergraduate Curriculum in Higher Education.* New York: Center for Applied Research in Education, 1963.

Education at Berkeley. Report of the Select Committee on Education (The Muscatine Report). Berkeley, Calif.: University of California Press, 1968.

Educational Facilities Laboratories. *To Build or Not to Build.* New York, n.d.

Ford Foundation. *Toward Greatness in Higher Education.* New York: Ford Foundation Office of Reports, 1964.

Gorovitz, Samuel (ed.). *Freedom and Order in the University.* Cleveland, Ohio: The Press of Western Reserve University, 1967.

Harris, Seymour E., Kenneth M. Deitch, and Alan Levensohn (eds.). *Challenge and Change in American Education.* Berkeley, Calif.: McCutchan, 1965.

Hofstadter, Richard, and Wilson Smith (eds.). *American Higher Education.* Vol. I. Chicago: University of Chicago Press, 1961.

Jencks, Christopher, and David Riesman. *The Academic Revolution.* Garden City, N.Y.: Doubleday, 1968.

Keeton, Morris, *Shared Authority on Campus,* Washington, D.C.: American Association for Higher Education, 1971.

Kerr, Clark. *The Uses of the University.* New York: Harper and Row, 1963.

McGrath, Earl J. *Memo to a College Faculty Member.* New York: Bureau of Publications, Teachers College, Columbia University, 1965.

Madsen, David. *The National University.* Detroit: Wayne State University, 1966.

Mayhew, Lewis B., *Arrogance on Campus.* San Francisco: Jossey-Bass, 1970.

Nance, Paul K., Leslie F. Robbins, and J. Harvey Cain. *Guide to College and University Business Management.* Washington, D.C.: U.S. Department of Health, Education, and Welfare, Office of Education, Bureau of Educational Research, 1965.

National Federation of College and University Business Officers Association. *Sixty College Study: A Second Look, the Sixty College Operating Data for 1957–1958.* Washington, D.C., 1960.

Pattillo, Manning M., Jr., and Donald M. Mackenzie. *Church-sponsored Higher Education in the United States.* Report of the Danforth Commission. Washington, D.C.: American Council on Education, 1966.

Paulsen, F. Robert. *American Education, Challenges and Images.* Tucson, Ariz.: University of Arizona Press, 1967.

Perkins, James A. *The University in Transition.* Princeton, N.J.: Princeton University Press, 1966.

Pfeiffer, John. *New Look at Education.* New York: Odyssey Press, 1968.

Rourke, Francis E., and Glenn E. Brooks. *The Managerial Revolution in Higher Education.* Baltimore: Johns Hopkins Press, 1967.

Rudolph, Frederick. *The American College and University.* New York: Alfred A. Knopf, 1965.

Ruml, Beardsley, and Donald H. Morrison. *Memo to a College Trustee.* New York: McGraw-Hill, 1959.

Sanford, Nevitt. *Where Colleges Fail.* San Francisco, Calif.: Jossey-Bass, 1967.

Scheps, Clarence. *Accounting for Colleges and Universities.* Baton Rouge, La.: Louisiana State University Press, 1949.

Smith, Huston. *The Purposes of Higher Education.* New York: Harper & Brothers, 1955.

Stroup, Thomas B. (ed.). *The University in the American Future.* Lexington, Ky.: University of Kentucky Press, 1965.

Thomas, Russell. *The Search for a Common Learning: General Education, 1800–1960.* New York: McGraw-Hill, 1962.

Tickton, Sidney G. *Needed: A Ten-Year College Budget.* New York: The Fund for the Advancement of Education, 1961.

Tiedt, Sidney W. *The Role of the Federal Government in Education.* New York: Oxford University Press, 1966.

U.S. National Student Association. *1967–1968 Codification of Policy.* Washington, D.C., 1967.

Whitehead, Alfred North. *The Aims of Education.* New York: Macmillan, 1929; reprinted, Mentor Book, New American Library of World Literature.

Williams, Harry. *Planning for Effective Resource Allocation in Universities.* Washington, D.C.: American Council on Education, 1966.

Wilson, Logan (ed.). *Emerging Patterns in American Higher Education.* Washington, D.C.: American Council on Education, 1965.

2. Articles and Unpublished or Limited-Circulation Documents

American Association of University Professors, the American Council on Education, and the Association of Governing Boards of Universities and Colleges. "Statement on Government of Colleges and Universities." Reprinted in the *Chronicle of Higher Education,* Jan. 1967; also reprinted by the University of Virginia Graduate School of Business Administration (UVA A&P-1) by permission of the *Chronicle of Higher Education.*

"Conversations toward a Definition of Institutional Vitality," Educational Testing Service, 1967.

Davis, Paul H. *Formula for Significant Survival of Private Liberal Arts Colleges.* Washington, D.C.: Council of Protestant Colleges and Universities, 1966. Monograph.

Doermann, Humphrey. "The Market for College Education." *Educational Record* (American Council on Education), Winter, 1968.

Dyer, Henry S. "Institutional Research and Measurement in Higher Education." Lecture given at an Educational Testing Service workshop on Institutional Research Programs. Lehigh University, Feb. 7, 1966.

Graese, C. E. "University Management—A Total Review," *Management Controls* (Peat, Marwick, Mitchell and Company), April 1968.

Hirschl, Harry H. "Some Economic Considerations and a Procedure for a University Cost Study." Master's thesis. Lafayette, Ind.: Purdue University, 1965.

Kershaw, Joseph A. "Long-Range Planning at Williams," *Williams Alumni Review,* May 1968.

The Report of the President. Yale University, 1967–1968.

"Running a University under Fire," *Business Week,* Sept. 1968.

Scheps, Clarence. "Is Higher Education in Financial Trouble?" Unpublished speech. Tulane University, 1967.

Turner, Lynn W. "Half-Way up Parnassus," *The Historian.* Nov. 1967.

U.S. Office of Education, Department of Health, Education, and Welfare.

Opening Fall Enrollment in Higher Education, 1967, and *Supplement A.* Washington, D.C.: Govt. Printing Office, 1967.

The University and Its Resources. Cambridge, Mass.: Harvard University Press, 1968.

Wess, Harold B. "Is Efficiency Taboo in Academia?" *Educational Record* (American Council on Education) Winter 1968.

Many published and unpublished documents from the participating institutions were used in this study including catalogs, bulletins, minutes of trustee meetings, and so on.

B. Business Sources

1. Books

Ansoff, H. Igor. *Corporate Strategy.* New York: McGraw-Hill, 1965.

Anthony, Robert N., John Dearden, and Richard F. Vancil. *Management Control Systems.* Homewood, Ill.: Richard D. Irwin, 1965.

Bacon, Jeremy. *Corporate Directorship Practices.* Business Policy Study no. 125. New York: National Industrial Conference Board, 1967.

Bierman, Jr., Harold, and Seymour Smidt. *The Capital Budgeting Decision.* New York: Macmillan, 1966.

Cannon, J. Thomas. *Business Strategy and Policy.* New York: Harcourt, Brace & World, 1968.

Chandler, Alfred D., Jr. *Strategy and Structure.* Cambridge, Mass.: M.I.T. Press, 1962.

Donaldson, Gordon. *Corporate Debt Capacity.* Boston: Division of Research, Graduate School of Business Administration, Harvard University, 1961.

Ginzberg, Eli, Dale H. Heistand, and Beatrice G. Reubins. *The Pluralistic Economy.* New York: McGraw-Hill, 1959.

Johnson, Robert W. *Financial Management.* 3rd ed. Boston: Allyn and Bacon, 1966.

Learned, Edmund P., *et al. Business Policy, Text and Cases.* Homewood, Ill.: Richard D. Irwin, 1965.

National Association of Accountants. *Financial Analysis to Guide Capital Expenditure Decisions.* Research Report no. 43. New York, 1967.

——. *Return on Capital as a Guide to Managerial Decisions.* Research Report no. 35. New York, 1959.

Solomon, Ezra. *The Theory of Financial Management.* New York: Columbia University Press, 1963.

Solomons, David. *Divisional Performance: Measurement of Control.* New York: Financial Executives Research Foundation, 1965.

2. *Articles and Cases*

"The Buckeye Pipe Line Company," ICH 9F104, Harvard Graduate School of Business Administration, 1964.

Childs, Wendell M. "Capital Budgeting for Improved Profits," *Management Accounting* (National Association of Accountants), May 1964.

"Frontier Rubber Company," ICH 4F68R, prepared by Joseph L. Fromm under the direction of Robert F. Vandell, Harvard Graduate School of Business Administration, 1959.

"General Holding Corporation," ICH 9F103, Harvard Graduate School of Business Administration, 1964.

Granger, Charles H. "The Hierarchy of Objectives," *Harvard Business Review*, May–June 1964.

Guth, W. D. "Personal Values and Corporate Strategy," ICH 10G11, Harvard Business School, 1963.

"The International Manufacturing Company" (B), ICH 9G250R, Harvard Business School, 1964.

Mace, Myles L., "The President and Corporate Planning," *Harvard Business Review*, Jan.–Feb. 1965.

Mainer, Robert. "The Case of the Stymied Strategist," *Harvard Business Review*, May–June 1968.

Meyers, Ronald E. "Performance Review of Capital Expenditures," *Management Accounting* (National Association of Accountants), Dec. 1966.

"Molecular Compounds Corporation" (abridged), ICH 10F88, Harvard Graduate School of Business Administration, 1962.

Rotch, William, "United Electronics Corporation" (A) and (B), UVA-C-355 and 359, Sponsors of the Graduate School of Business Administration, University of Virginia, 1966.

Sawyers, William E. "Capital Budgeting of Oil Pipe Lines," *Management Accounting* (National Association of Accountants), May 1964.

Smalter, Donald J., and Rudy L. Ruggles. "Six Business Lessons from the Pentagon," *Harvard Business Review*, March–April 1966.

Tilles, Seymour. "How to Evaluate Corporate Strategy," *Harvard Business Review*, July–August 1963.

———. "The Manager's Job—A Systems Approach," *Harvard Business Review*, Jan.–Feb. 1963.

———. "Strategies for Allocating Funds," *Harvard Business Review*, Jan.–Feb. 1966.

Usry, Milton F. "A Capital Expenditure Framework," *Management Accounting* (National Association of Accountants), Nov. 1964.

Vandell, Robert F. "Consolidated Electrical Products, Inc." (A) through (E), ICH 4F78, Harvard College, 1958–59.

——. "Note on the Capital Allocation Process," UVA-F-121, Sponsors of the Graduate School of Business Administration, University of Virginia, 1966.